'WELL WORTH THE WAIT

'WELL WORTH THE WAIT

The Story of Motherwell's Epic Cup Triumph

JOHN SWINBURNE

MAINSTREAM
PUBLISHING

EDINBURGH AND LONDON

Copyright © John Swinburne 1991

First published in Great Britain 1991 by
MAINSTREAM PUBLISHING COMPANY (EDINBURGH)
LTD
7 Albany Street
Edinburgh EH1 3UG

ISBN 1 85158 447 1 (paper)

A catalogue record for this book is available from the
British Library

Typeset in 11/13pt Sabon
Printed in Great Britain by
Butler & Tanner Ltd, Frome and London

To Tommy McLean, with grateful thanks
Also to Laura, my daughter, who kept me on schedule
Finally, to the Motherwell players and their
magnificent supporters

Thanks again for the memories

CONTENTS

ACKNOWLEDGMENTS

The black and white photographs in this book have been supplied by Charlie McBain, regional chief photographer of Scottish Universal Newspapers, who has been a life-long supporter of the club. He even played a trial for the 'Well prior to being called up to do his National Service.

Charlie took great pleasure in Motherwell's Cup win and every player plus the management team received an envelope containing photographs of the great event. Each player will cherish this generous act in the years to come. The quality of his shots are superb.

He contributed to the last book I wrote which marked the club's centenary and his library of past players is very extensive.

I am indebted to Charlie for his co-operation in providing these photographs and also to Bob Wyper who supplied the colour shots for the cover of the book.

Craig Halkett, by courtesy of the *Daily Record*, also obliged by allowing me to use some of his photographs of the 'Magnificent Seven' survivors of the 1952 final, plus a few others. These were in superb colour but unfortunately costs dictate that they must be reproduced in black and white. I would also like to thank Jim Jeffrey for statistical assistance.

Tommy McLean in 1984

FOREWORD

It was around Christmas 1981 that John Chapman was co-opted on to the Board of Directors of Motherwell Football Club. It took him until 1989 to turn the club around financially. He was, of course, ably assisted by Tommy McLean who was appointed as team manager in June 1984. Tommy's astute dealings in the transfer market have obviously helped the club to become established financially.

Very few know the real story of financial planning and astute budgeting which John Chapman instituted. He ensured that every detail, no matter how small, was dealt with to the club's financial advantage.

In these troubled financial times, Motherwell are now in the élite band of football clubs who can boast that they are operating in the black. Debt and soccer have become synonymous, with inflated transfer fees being equated with, or perhaps I should say confused with, football ability. Does ANYONE seriously believe that 'Gazza' is worth all those millions? No one would question his soccer ability or that he knows the correct time to shed a tear or two but he has been hyped up by the media out of all proportion.

To return to the original topic – John Chapman and Tommy McLean are now reaping the rewards of a long, long period of hard work in the process of which they have turned Motherwell Football Club from an ailing team into one which is a match for any in the country.

It certainly has been a long hard road and I would like to go on record here and now and thank John Chapman for saving our club and Tommy McLean for giving Motherwell fans back their pride.

The words in this foreword first appeared in our match programme of 4 May 1991 for the Motherwell v Rangers game, which incidentally Motherwell won by three goals to nil and in the process blew the race for the league championship wide open. The facts are even more true now, after Motherwell's Cup victory over Dundee United, than they were when they were originally written.

I feel that it is right and fitting that this piece is used as a foreword to a book which shows the progress of the club since the time that Tommy McLean took over as manager.

JOHN SWINBURNE

INTRODUCTION

By Tommy McLean

I am delighted that after seven years of hard work once again Motherwell Football Club have achieved success and won a major trophy, after a long spell during which no honours came their way.

It has been very difficult at times because of the financial restraints but this only makes it all the more rewarding. The fans have been magnificent in the way that they rallied round to support the club, and with six weeks to go before the new season gets underway it is tremendous to hear that we have already sold four times as many season tickets as last season.

The players responded to the challenge and proved to everybody that they were worthy winners of the Scottish Cup.

This book will deal with the Cup victory in depth and I am pleased that it all worked out for everyone attached to the club as well as it did.

For me the most rewarding feature was seeing all the young boys who started on the Youth Training Scheme developing over the years, coming good on the day and winning winners medals.

Our Cup victory has pushed the club into the European scene – a new area for Motherwell FC which introduces a whole new dimension which we gladly welcome.

Tommy McLean being interviewed after the final

Chapter One

REALISATION

'YES!' was the cry. Hands held aloft, thousands of fans were jumping up and down in the confined space allowed between the rows of seats at Hampden. They embraced all and sundry in a state of pure, unadulterated ecstasy and joy.

The time was 5.22 p.m. on the afternoon of 18 May 1991. David Syme, the referee, had just blown his whistle to bring to an end one of the hardest fought contests since the Scottish Cup was first instituted back in 1874. In all those years there had never been a finer contest than that between Dundee United and Motherwell. The realisation that Motherwell had won the Cup exploded upon the reality of the massed 'Well fans, and the exuberant celebrations which followed were the ultimate outcome of 39 years of hope followed by frustration and failure.

At that moment, however, nothing else mattered. Football is an 'escapist' sport – for 90 minutes, if the game is good enough, fans can forget the often daunting and depressing realities of life and concentrate upon the drama which invariably unfolds in every football match played in the right competitive manner.

To use an engineering expression, over the years I had become 'case-hardened' against defeat. I had found out many years ago that football can be quite a cruel and heart-breaking sport. Unless you accepted the fact that defeat in any game can be the final outcome then you simply could never survive as a soccer fan. You have to learn to take the good with the bad. In the past decades, to be honest, there has been much more to be disappointed about than to celebrate. It has not been easy to support Motherwell throughout those lean years but some of us have persevered.

While every Motherwell fan at Hampden that May day felt elation as the adrenalin went pumping through their system, it was that extra bit special for those who had suffered longest.

Meanwhile, the antics of the players on the park were a joy to behold as they, even more than the fans, celebrated their hard-won victory.

Among the supporters, some shed tears. Some just sat shaking their heads in disbelief. Some sang and cheered while some danced like demented dervishes.

Motherwell had won the Cup in a match of unprecedented tension and drama. At that precise moment in time all was well with the world and nothing else on earth was of any consequence.

What a climax to any competition this had turned out to be. The advantage went from one side to the other and at all times the calibre of the play was of the highest order. There had been seven goals and any one of them would have been fit to win a game. But this match was more than a little bit special – this was the game which had been chosen to show to all and sundry just what a superb spectacle soccer can be. This game probably did more to restore the faith of countless thousands in football as the ultimate spectator sport than any other in recent years.

It is always nice to win, but when you win in a manner which makes you the talking point of the country then you know you have experienced a rare sensation – exactly the sensation that every Motherwell player enjoyed at 5.22 p.m. on 18 May 1991.

Chapter Two

STABILITY

When Tommy McLean took over at Motherwell and I met him for the first time, I congratulated him on his appointment and stated that I hoped his stay would be a long one because Motherwell Football Club was sorely in need of stability.

I pointed out to Tommy that he was the *ninth* manager that the club had appointed in the last 11 years. This, in my opinion, had been the road to ruin because every new manager wanted to bring in his own players and get rid of the ones he had inherited. Stability was most certainly the missing ingredient at Fir Park.

Tommy is now about to enter his eighth season in charge of Motherwell FC. He has been a director of the club for three years. Motherwell FC is operating 'in the black' and we have won the Scottish Cup. We are in Europe for the first time in our history and while many have contributed to this success story in some small or large measure, Tommy McLean is entitled to the lion's share of praise because he has done exactly what I had hoped he would do. He has brought STABILITY to Motherwell Football Club.

Another indicator of the influence of Tommy McLean is the comparison between the club's financial position in 1984 and 1991. From over £800,000 in debt to an undisclosed amount in credit. What a turnabout in the club's fortunes.

Tommy would be the last to claim all the credit for this transformation. However, there is no denying the fact that he was certainly the prime reason for the improvement with his astute dealings in the transfer market. He would probably say that there

17

Stability is – a Cup-winning squad

were many other factors and that there was a great deal of teamwork involved in bringing about this mini-miracle. It is indeed miraculous in these times when many clubs associate success with huge overdrafts and think that to be successful you must be seen to be bidding for or buying players for ludicrously inflated transfer fees. Very few could have achieved what Tommy McLean has achieved within the financial restraints imposed on him.

I have no doubt that Tommy will continue to be 'careful' in his purchasing of players but I am happy in the knowledge that if or when he decides to purchase a player for a fee which he thinks is fair, the money is there to cover the cost of his purchase. Changed days indeed from the time, for example, that the club simply couldn't refuse a £90,000 offer from Celtic for Brian McClair in 1982. We all know that Manchester United forked out ten times that figure to obtain the services of Brian McClair a few years later. In 1982 if the bank said sell, you simply HAD to sell. It is nice to be out of that type of situation and be masters of our own destiny once more. Stability has returned to Fir Park and at the end of the day the fans must be the winners because we will be watching a far more stable team.

Chapter Three

THE MANAGER

Tommy McLean has an impeccable footballing background. Born in Ashgill in 1947, he was drawn into football because his two older brothers, Willie and Jim, were both professionals.

Tommy started his career with Birkenshaw Amateurs and he was only 15 when he signed for Kilmarnock in 1962. He was an orthodox right winger of the highest calibre in his early days at Rugby Park and he had tremendous 'vision' and the uncanny ability to pin-point his crosses with unerring accuracy.

Tommy was capped as an amateur and also at Youth level and he didn't have to wait long before he tasted success. In 1965 he won his first League Championship medal when he helped Killie pip Hearts on goal average at Tynecastle on the very last game of the League campaign.

His manager at that time was the great Willie Waddell and not surprisingly when Waddell moved on to Ibrox one of his first signings, for a fee of £75,000, was Tommy McLean.

In his successful footballing career Tommy won seven full Scotland caps and a couple of Under-21 caps. He added to his Kilmarnock League Championship medal at Ibrox by winning another three League Championship medals, four Scottish Cup Winners medals and two League Cup Winners medals. Over and above all that he also won a European Cup Winners Cup medal.

When he hung up his boots he moved into management as assistant manager under John Greig, and when John resigned he moved in the middle of season 1983/84 to Cappielow as assistant to his former team-mate, Alex Miller. Tommy took control at Morton when Alex Miller moved to Paisley.

He quickly guided the Cappielow team to promotion to the Premier League and surprised some people when he opted to leave promoted Morton to take over the relegated Motherwell side. At the time, he stated that he felt that there was more potential at Motherwell despite the fact that they were over £800,000 in debt and obviously in a demoralised state after suffering relegation a mere two years after Davie Hay won promotion for them in the 1981/82 season.

With no funds with which to buy players, Tommy McLean had a gargantuan task on his hands. During the summer shut-down he had to sell both Stuart Rafferty to Dundee and Kenny Black to Hearts. Despite this he astutely moulded together a team which, after a shaky start, consolidated, and not only won the First Division Championship but also fought their way through to the semi-final of the Scottish Cup where they held Celtic to a 1–1 draw before going down 3–0 in the replay.

There were a fair number of signings and departures as Tommy scoured the First Division for suitably priced players. Even the transfer of Gary McAllister and Ally Mauchlen to Leicester City for a quarter of a million pounds did little to ease Tommy's problems with regard to signing players, because this sum was quickly gobbled up by the banks to help ease the overdraft situation.

A youth policy was set up by Tommy and he stated then that this would take at least five years to bear fruit. In the meantime, players continued to come and go as he strove to attain survival at Premier League level. It must have been heartbreaking to lose quality players such as Fraser Wishart and Andy Walker but he compensated by signing others such as Stevie Kirk, Tam McAdam, Paul Kinnaird, Stevie Cowan, Raymond Farningham, Crawford Baptie, Paul Smith and a host of others including Bobby Russell and Craig Paterson.

He 'inherited' around 30 players, and over and above that number a grand total of 77 players have been signed by Tommy McLean since his arrival from Morton, and that does not include young 'S' form players who have come through from the youth policy.

On the other hand, 74 players have been transferred from

Can you pick out a young Phil O'Donnell? The early days of the youth policy which Tommy McLean set up. Bobby Jenks is seated second from the right

A young Gary McAllister

Motherwell or freed. To be fair, the turnover rate has slowed down dramatically in the past couple of seasons. I think it would be true to say that Tommy has enjoyed success this season with the *fifth* team which he has built during his seven-year term in office as manager and now director of Motherwell Football Club.

During this time Tommy's astute wheeling and dealing in the transfer market has resulted in Motherwell's overdraft being completely wiped out. He must take most of the credit for the fact that Motherwell Football Club have been operating in the black for the past two years.

Without question, Tommy's master stroke was when he signed Davie Cooper for a mere £50,000.

At times, Tommy McLean has been criticised by sections of the media, and on more than one occasion by Graeme Souness, for alleged negative play – particularly at Ibrox. All he was doing in actual fact was using the players available to him in the best possible way to obtain a positive result.

Few 'Well fans will fail to recall the 1–0 victory over Rangers when Ray Farningham scored in the 88th minute of the game and emptied Ibrox park in about 30 seconds flat! More recently, few 'Well fans will fail to recall the 3–0 defeat of Rangers in May 1991, a mere week or two after Graeme Souness emigrated to England. After all the jibes about negative play this result was gratefully received and it was a clear indicator of the greater success which lay ahead for Motherwell a couple of weeks later at Hampden Park.

It was easy for Souness to criticise Motherwell's tactics but, as I once heard a 'Well fan say, 'Tommy McLean could easily do Graeme Souness's job at Ibrox but could Souness do Tommy McLean's job at Motherwell on a shoestring?'

The team which Tommy McLean fielded at Hampden on 18 May 1991 had cost the club only £435,000. Craig Paterson was bought from Rangers for £25,000, Luc Nijholt came from Switzerland for £100,000, Iain Ferguson came from Hearts for £100,000, Davie Cooper was a 'steal' at £50,000, while super sub Stevie Kirk came to Fir Park for £65,000 (part of which was paid for by the transfer of Blair to East Fife), Ian Angus from Dundee cost £80,000 and finally Colin O'Neill cost only £15,000 from Portadown. This is a remarkable achievement in an era when individual players in Scotland cost as much as three times the total

Davie Cooper shows his new colours after signing for Motherwell

value paid for the whole of the Motherwell Scottish Cup winning side – including the substitutes.

Talking about substitutes, I feel very strongly that a rule change is urgently needed for the Scottish Cup final. It is high time that both competing teams (in the final only) were allowed to nominate five substitutes instead of the two which are permitted at present. Only two subs from five would be allowed to actually play, but in this way the managers would be spared the traumatic job on the eve of the final of telling members of his main squad, which usually numbers around 16, that they would not be selected to play.

Everyone's heart went out to John Philliben, for example. He had been a tower of strength at Aberdeen and also against Celtic in the semi-final. Wouldn't it have been nice to see him on the bench and therefore qualifying for the medal which he so richly deserved? As I said to John after the final in an attempt to console him when he returned to Fir Park, 'John, always remember we

23

wouldn't have won the Cup if it hadn't been for your efforts in the earlier rounds.'

Yes indeed, if a pool of substitutes is acceptable at International level then it is high time that 16 medals were automatically struck for the winning POOL of players in the Scottish Cup final.

At any rate, events were to prove that Tommy McLean made the correct choice when he came to manage Motherwell, but it was certainly no easy task that he undertook. He is now entitled to look back and give that quiet characteristic nod of satisfaction at the progress of his team to date. Always a winner, Tommy will not be satisfied to rest on his laurels. A perfectionist, he will continue to strive against all the odds and he will not be content until he has HIS team playing HIS own brand of football and he will never be satisfied with second best.

He has the knack of taking good players who have suffered a set-back in their playing careers and providing them with the challenge to start again and become better players. He can also squeeze an extra couple of great seasons out of great players who thought that they had had their day and were pleased to be given the opportunity to prove that they weren't finished yet. George Burley, Tam McAdam and Robert Russell fall into that category – as for Davie Cooper, everyone who loves football simply hopes that he will go on for ever!

Chapter Four

BIG TAM

Tom Forsyth has come a long way since signing for Bobby Howitt, the manager of Motherwell, away back in 1967. He soon established himself in Motherwell's team and in his early days he proved to be a very versatile player. Eventually, after spells as an inside forward, he stepped back to play in the number four jersey. He was capped for Scotland before moving on to Rangers in 1972.

There he was given a more defensive role and picked up a series of Scottish caps. He also played in the Argentine for Ally McLeod's squad. In all he was capped for his country 23 times.

It was at Ibrox that he first teamed up with Tommy McLean, both on and off the park. Being near neighbours, they travelled together and a close partnership was struck up which prevails to this day.

Big Tam played in no fewer than six Cup Finals, winning four and losing two. He will long be remembered for his late winning goal in that final against Celtic. He relished the atmosphere of Cup final days and he was determined that his squad would also relish their big day on 18 May 1991. It is an interesting fact that the second-in-command at Tannadice, Paul Sturrock, was always a difficult opponent for Tam to handle but he generally managed to come out on top in those encounters.

Tam Forsyth was one of the finest tacklers ever produced in Scotland and his timing was superb. At Ibrox he was regarded by some as a hard player. In his opinion there is no other way to play

The partners – Tommy McLean and Tam Forsyth

the game but he combined this with a basic fairness. Probably his greatest asset was his instinctive positional sense which made him a master of his craft.

Since teaming up in management with Tommy McLean they have gone from strength to strength, and with this Cup victory for Motherwell under their belts they can now aim for even greater achievements.

Tommy McLean tells a good story about the hardest half-back line he ever saw in his life – it was Tam Forsyth, Jim Holton and Willie McVie. The mind boggles at the thought but they did play together and I presume that Tommy McLean was a spectator that day or he probably wouldn't have survived to tell the tale!

'How did the 1991 final compare with your other Cup final matches?' I enquired of Tam.

'Sheer murder,' he answered. 'The frustration that you feel in the dugout is the worst feeling in the world. At least on the other times when I was involved, I was on the park where I could do something about the game and influence it directly, but when you're sitting watching and can't do anything it is sheer murder.

'A Cup final is the worst game of all to lose. I have always been a bad loser and I impressed upon the boys that after going so far they might just as well go the whole road and win.

'I was delighted for each and every one of them because they really worked hard for each other and deserved their victory.

'Defeat was unthinkable – three months is a long time to lick your wounds before you can get another game under your belt.'

Yes indeed, Big Tam is and always has been an out and out winner and he obviously got his message across to his team.

John C. Chapman, Chairman of Motherwell Football Club

Chapter Five

THE BOARD

Motherwell Football Club have been operating for the past few years with a three-man Board of Directors. John Chapman is the chairman, Bill Dickie is the vice-chairman and Tommy McLean is the third member of the triumvirate.

Club chairman John Chapman is inclined by nature to be rather reticent. He is well known throughout Scotland in the meat trade. He is the managing director of a business which covers a range of shops in Wishaw and Motherwell as well as an abattoir and a farm. As mentioned in the foreword of this book, he joined the board of Motherwell FC late in 1981.

Never one to shirk a challenge, John Chapman set about the unenviable task of putting the club on a sound financial footing. After eight very difficult years he saw the club turn the corner financially. Two years later he has been repaid for all his arduous efforts and worry by seeing his club achieve its first major success since 1952.

'It was a Wishaw man who was chairman the last time that we won the Cup,' was one of his comments as he accepted congratulations from all and sundry on his return to Fir Park after the big game.

I was waiting for him at the top of the stairs outside the board room when he arrived back on the team bus. I congratulated him and presented him with a beautiful ship's decanter engraved with the Motherwell logo, and below the club's crest were the engraved words: 'MOTHERWELL FOOTBALL CLUB – SCOTTISH CUP

John Chapman (extreme left) even took a back seat on the celebration bus tour

WINNERS 1991'. Mark you, this was only about 90 minutes after the final whistle! Raymond Davidson had given me the decanter about two weeks before the final with the instructions that in the unlikely event of the 'Well suffering a defeat, 'Drown your sorrows and throw the decanter away.'

Well, Raymond, the decanter, which is still filled with 21-year-old Bowmore single malt whisky, will be opened on the next occasion that Motherwell win a major trophy. One thing is certain: it will not take another 39 years before the club has cause to celebrate.

Vice-President of Motherwell FC Bill Dickie, also SFA Vice-President

The players and the trophy arrived back at Fir Park minus Maxie, who had been taken to the Victoria Infirmary, and Ian Angus, who had been held back to undergo a drugs test. They all went into the directors' box to salute the fans who were singing and cheering on the park.

John Chapman was a happy man – not so much for himself as for the fans, the players and the club, and especially for Tommy McLean who had worked so hard for Motherwell and who really deserved a break.

Mr. W. H. Dickie RIBA is the vice-chairman of Motherwell Football and Athletic Club. He is also the senior vice-president of the Scottish Football Association and he should take over the position of president in 1994 after Peter Gardiner has served his four-year term of office.

Bill Dickie has been a director of Motherwell FC for 15 years and he has served in many capacities on the Scottish Football League Management Committee as well as at the SFA for most of that time. He is also a past chairman of Motherwell FC and he

31

was the founder chairman of the Fir Park Vice-Presidents Club in 1972.

Bill was born in Law and he started his own architect's business 27 years ago. He has seen many changes at the top at Fir Park over the years and he is thoroughly delighted that the team triumphed at Hampden on 18 May.

Chapter Five

SEVEN SEASONS TO SUCCESS

1984/85

Tommy McLean took over as manager in June 1984. With his consent the directors had sold both Kenny Black to Hearts and Stuart Rafferty to Dundee before he actually took up office at Fir Park.

It is interesting to look at the pool of players which won the First Division Championship. Of the 24 players who played for Motherwell in the season 1984/85 only Alastair Maxwell, who was Tommy's original choice for the number one jersey and who managed 15 appearances in that campaign, survived right up until the start of season 1991/92. Tommy Boyd, who left for Chelsea in May 1991 after leading the 'Well to their Cup victory, notched a good solid 35 games plus one sub appearance in season 1984/85.

In November 1984, Tommy made one of his quite frequent calls to Jim McLean and signed John Gardiner for a fee of around £10,000. Jamie Doyle put in an appearance in early December from Partick Thistle and he managed 15 games. It is interesting now to look back on how the player pool was made up.

Alastair Maxwell played 15 games, John Gardiner, 24 games and Andy Dornan, 18 games plus three as sub. He scored one goal against Falkirk. Derek Murray was another arrival from Dundee United and he played in 34 games and scored on five occasions. Big Graeme Forbes was played at the heart of the defence. He managed 34 full games plus two sub appearances and on his regular forays up the park at set pieces, Graeme scored a total of four goals.

Big Gregor Stevens briefly came and went after only eight games; Tommy moved him on to Thistle in a swop deal involving Jamie Doyle. Gregor had been previously at Fir Park under Willie McLean, and Ally McLeod had sold him to Leicester City for £120,000. From Leicester he moved to Rangers before his short sojourn at his old stamping ground of Fir Park.

Ian MacLeod was nearly an ever-present with a solid 38 matches to his credit. He only missed out on the Meadowbank game in April 1985. Ian McDonald was another player signed by Tommy and given an early chance to shine. He was part of the Jamie Doyle deal in mid-season after ten games plus three sub appearances and four goals.

The elegant Gary McAllister was quickly picked out by Tommy McLean as being 'the best prospect in the squad'. Although he was only 19 years of age he had, and indeed still has, a beautiful touch on the ball. Listed as being 5ft 10in and 9½ stone in weight, Gary has since filled out to achieve his full potential. He is currently in Andy Roxburgh's plans and is being capped regularly for his country. Leeds paid over £1,000,000 for his transfer from Leicester City. In season 1984/85 he played in 34 matches plus one sub appearance and scored six league goals.

Rab Stewart was signed by Tommy from Dunfermline and managed 22 games plus four times on the bench to score nine league goals. Veteran Andy Harrow also scored nine league goals and he was 37 times (once as a sub) on duty for the 'Well.

Kenny Lyall had been signed from Rangers in a double deal when Bobby Watson had also signed Kenny Black. Young Lyall only managed two games under Tommy McLean. Paul McFadden was one of the spare strikers and he scored twice in the promotion campaign in his two appearances. He was six times on the bench.

Ian Alexander, who had been signed by Jock Wallace, failed to establish himself under Tommy McLean. He had five games and three as sub and notched a single goal, while the popular Johnny Gahagan had 17 games plus 14 sub appearances and scored five valuable league goals.

Ally Mauchlen had 29 games to his credit plus one on the bench and he scored one goal. He was the team captain and he led by example. A great competitor.

Mike Cormack quickly departed the scene after two sub appearances and one game in which he scored a thundering goal against

Motherwell winning the League Championship in season 1984/85

Ayr United. Raymond Blair was signed from St Johnstone and he managed to score six goals in his 21 games plus ten on the bench.

Robert Clark, who came from Kilmarnock in a swap deal involving Mike Cormack, had eight games and two as sub and scored in his debut against Meadowbank. Alex Kennedy was given a run in midfield but despite scoring a couple of goals in his 14 games (and two as sub) he never fully established himself in the team.

Tommy had been nursing Andy Walker along in the reserve team and he scored three goals from four games plus seven sub appearances. John McStay was another who broke through, and the big versatile Larkhall boy had the glory of scoring the goal which clinched promotion back to the Premier League when Motherwell beat Partick Thistle 1–0 on 20 April 1985.

During season 1984/85 Motherwell won more games than any other team in the First Division. They won a total of 21 of their 39 League Championship matches.

Season tickets were £60 for the stand and £35 for the ground. Admission to the stand in 1984/85 was £3.50 and an adult gained entry to the terracing for £2.

In the 1984/85 Skol Cup, Motherwell made an early exit at Ayr when they lost 1–0 to a John Murphy goal. However, Tommy's squad acquitted themselves very well in the Scottish Cup in his first season in charge. They beat Dumbarton 4–0 in the third round before dealing competently with Meadowbank Thistle by beating them 2–0 in the fourth round. Drawn at home against Forfar Athletic in the fifth round, the 'Well won 4–1. This qualified them to play Celtic in the semi-final and Gary McAllister stunned the Celtic fans by scoring an early goal. Celtic equalised, but who will ever forget that late header by big Graeme Forbes which beat everyone and just flashed past the wrong side of the post? In the replay Celtic made no mistake and won 3–0, to go on and win the Cup against Dundee United by 2–1. It is interesting to note that six years later only Maurice Malpas was selected to play in the final against Motherwell from that defeated Dundee United side.

Thus ended Tommy's first full season as manager of Motherwell Football Club. He had taken over a very demoralised club which had just been relegated and he had breathed new life into it. Privately he would probably have settled for another year in the First Division in order to allow him to consolidate, but he accepted the challenge of the Premier League with minimal funds and many positions urgently requiring to be strengthened.

The 1985/86 season would be make or break for Motherwell.

1985/86

Leicester City made a move in August 1985 for both Ally Mauchlen and Gary McAllister. A fee of £250,000 was agreed and this enabled Tommy McLean to give the club breathing space as far as the bank overdraft was concerned.

It was to be a very traumatic season for Motherwell. Their away record was the worst in Scotland. They recorded only three draws away from home and failed to win a single away League game.

In the Skol Cup they defeated Partick Thistle by 1–0 with Alex Kennedy scoring, before being thrashed 6–1 by Hibernian at Easter Road in the third round. Andy Harrow scored first and then the roof fell in, with Stevie Cowan scoring twice, Gordon Durie notching a hat-trick and Joe McBride claiming a single.

Graeme Forbes, who nearly took us to the final in 1985

The Scottish Cup was little better. 'Well beat Brechin City 2–0 after two 1–1 games. Next they beat Alloa 2–1 at Recreation Park before losing by the only goal of the game against Dundee United in the fifth round.

New faces in the claret and amber in 1985/86 included Jim Clark with five games, Chris McCart with 11 games and one as sub, Jim Weir with two games and one as sub, and John Reilly, a £50,000 signing from Dundee United, who played in 24 games plus six as sub, scoring nine goals in the process. Brian Wright was signed from Hamilton Academicals. He filled the number 10 jersey on 28 occasions and scored six goals.

Fraser Wishart made his debut and played exceptionally soundly at both left and right back in 26 matches. Frank Mulveney was signed from Forth Wanderers and played in four matches plus one sub appearance. Crawford Baptie was signed from Falkirk and he contributed three goals to our modest total from 14 games, with another two as sub. Jim Griffin made his debut against Hibs in his only game with the big team, and Martin McBride was substitute against Hibs in the third last game of the season.

Yes, 1985/86 was an extremely difficult season. For the second time in their 100-year history, re-organisation of the league set-up had come to Motherwell's rescue and saved them from plunging back down into the obscurity of the First Division and probable financial ruin. Former chairman Ian Livingstone must take a great deal of credit for bringing about this state of affairs.

Tommy McLean had lost two of his key men in Mauchlen and McAllister before the season got properly underway. This tore the heart out of his midfield and this season was the first in the club's history that they failed to record an away victory. Injuries and suspensions also made life extremely difficult, and on no fewer than 16 occasions the team were within one goal of gaining a favourable result but of course this is normally regarded as classic relegation form.

Tommy Boyd was the fans' choice as 'Player of the Year' and other youngsters were introduced during the season.

1986/87

The highlight of the 1986/87 season was without doubt the visit of English League Champions and FA Cup Winners, Liverpool,

Tommy McLean's squad for the 1985/86 season: (left to right) Top:
*McCart, Clark, Kennedy, McAllister, McKeown, Gardiner, Maxwell,
Forbes, MacLeod, McStay, Allan;* Middle: *Blair, Dornan, Griffin,
Boyd, Diver, McLean, McBride, McFadden, Stewart, Doyle, Findlay;*
Bottom: *Gary McKenzie (physio), Wishart, Gahagan, Harrow,
T. McLean, T. Forsyth, Mauchlen, Walker, Murray, O'Hare, Doyle,
C. Murray (coach)*

led by 'King' Kenny Dalglish, to play Motherwell in a match to
celebrate the centenary of the 'Steelmen'.

Tommy McLean introduced another new batch of players,
including Paul Smith from Raith Rovers, Gordon Mair from
Lincoln City, Gary Fraser from Queen's Park, Stevie Kirk from
East Fife, John Philliben from Doncaster, Ray Farningham from
Forfar and Tom McAdam from Hamilton Academicals. Young
Neil Candlish stepped up from the YTS ranks, Craig Paterson
was signed from Rangers, Dougie Arnott arrived from Pollock
Juniors, and Kevin McKeown, a young goalkeeper, was also given
a game.

Tommy also appointed Bobby Jenks to organise his youth
policy as head scout, and the Motherwell Boys' Club will pay
dividends in the future. The 21-year lease by the Fir Park Social
Club came to an end and they were moved over to Edward Street.
This enabled a far more professional approach to the running of
a Premier League club to be adopted. For example, a new office
complex was built under the stand.

Motherwell completed the season in eighth place in the Premier League. In the Scottish Cup they disposed of Partick Thistle at Fir Park by 3–1 and beat Hamilton Accies away from home by 2–1 before drawing with Hearts 1–1 and eventually going down in the replay by 1–0.

It was in the Skol Cup that a taste of glory was within their reach. The 'Well disposed of Arbroath by 4–0 in the second round, they beat Clydebank by 2–0 in the third round and Forfar were their victims in the fourth round by 2–1. In the semi-final against Celtic the scoreline stood at 2–2 after extra time, with the 'Well goals coming from Andy Walker and Paul Smith. Brian McClair and Roy Aitken scored for Celtic. In the penalty shoot-out, Celtic won by 5–4, when John Philliben nearly broke the crossbar as he missed with his attempt.

The highlight of the whole season was the 1–0 defeat of Rangers on 8 November 1986. Ray Farningham 'emptied' Ibrox in 30 seconds flat with his 88th-minute winning goal.

Andy Walker moved to Celtic during the summer break for £375,000.

1987/88

Probably the most significant signings were Cameron Duncan, a goalkeeper from Sunderland, Paul Kinnaird from Dundee United, Stevie Cowan from Hibs, Robert Russell from Rangers and Jamie Fairlie from Clydebank.

This was a traumatic season with three teams being relegated to allow the Premier League to revert to a ten-team set-up. Motherwell, with 11 points from their last eight games, finished the season in eighth position to consolidate their place in the Premier League.

The problems of season 1987/88 were obvious for all to see. A regular goalscorer was urgently required. With only 37 goals from 44 games to our credit we were indeed fortunate that our defence conceded very little in any game, losing only 55 goals in the whole League programme. Tom McAdam and Craig Paterson blended well at the heart of the defence.

At Easter Road on 23 April 1988, Fraser Wishart limped off the park with six minutes to go, thus breaking his record of having played 101 consecutive League games. During season

Stevie Cowan, who was Motherwell's top scorer in 1987/88 with nine goals

1986/87 he was the only outfield player in the Premier League to play a full 90 minutes in each of the 44 league matches.

The 1987 Skol Cup saw Motherwell beat Airdrie by 3–1 at Fir Park. The goals were scored by Gordon Mair, Jamie Fairlie and Tom Boyd. Davie McCabe scored Airdrie's goal. A 4–0 defeat of Albion Rovers, with the goals by Stevie Kirk, Robert Russell (two) and an Edgar own-goal, saw Motherwell through to a fourth round tie against Hibs on Tuesday, 1 September 1987. Jamie Fairlie scored the only goal of the game and our next tie was the semi-final against Rangers at Hampden on 23 September. Paul Smith scored to give Motherwell an early lead but a crazy two-minute spell just before half-time saw an own goal by Stevie Kirk and a soft goal by Fleck take Rangers into the lead. They clung on to this lead until Falco scored in the 89th minute to make the final score 3–1.

In the 1988 Scottish Cup, Motherwell eased through by 3–1 against Kilmarnock after a 0–0 draw at Fir Park, only to go down to Dundee by 2–0 at Dens Park. Former 'Well favourite Stewart Rafferty scored for Dundee and Ian Angus made it 2–0.

1988/89

This was the season in which Chris McCart established himself as a first team regular. He managed 25 games plus one sub selection. Robert Russell shook off niggling injuries to score five goals in his 28 games. He was also sub on three occasions. Paul Smith and Raymond Farningham moved to Dunfermline. Stevie Kirk scored 14 league goals from midfield. Paul Kinnaird moved to St Mirren for £80,000 – good business, as Tommy bought him for £20,000. Dave McCabe found Premier League goals much harder to score than First Division goals.

Stevie Bryce was given three games plus six substitute appearances. Alex Kennedy moved to Firhill. Maxie re-established himself as the number one goalkeeper at Fir Park and Jamie Dolan was introduced into the squad. Most notably, however, Colin O'Neill was signed from Portadown for a mere £15,000. He played in 19 games and scored two goals and he instantly became a firm favourite with the fans.

In the Skol Cup we beat Airdrie in the second round by an extra-time goal from Ray Farningham. We took an early exit at

*Stevie Kirk and David Robertson joust for the ball. Stevie was the
1988/99 top 'Well scorer*

the hands of Dunfermline by 2–1 at East End Park. Stevie Kirk
was our scorer.

In the Scottish Cup we eliminated Falkirk at Fir Park by 2–1

43

after squeezing a 1–1 draw at Falkirk. Stevie Kirk scored our three goals against the Bairns. In the fourth round we went down to Hibs at Easter Road. The highlight of this game was a superb goal by substitute Stevie Bryce.

We squeezed into ninth position in the League and avoided the drop. The team was showing glimpses of consistency and better times seemed to lie ahead.

1989/90

Nicky Cusack, a six-foot striker from Peterborough United, was signed by Tommy McLean on 19 July 1989, and on 11 August 1989 Tommy made the most significant signing that he had made since taking over at Fir Park. He signed Davie Cooper from Rangers for a fee of £50,000.

Other recruits were George Burley on a free transfer to replace Fraser Wishart who had moved to St Mirren for a fee which was set by the tribunal at £287,000. Tom McAdam moved on to Airdrie as a player-coach after serving Motherwell exceptionally well in his spell with the Fir Park side.

Davie Cooper played in 31 games and scored six goals. Nicky Cusack found the target on 11 occasions and played in 29 matches plus two substitute appearances. Maxie was an ever-present in goal and he had nine League shut-outs. Stevie Kirk scored eight League goals and Dougie Arnott was another to benefit from the superb service being provided by Davie Cooper, aided and abetted by Bobby Russell.

The crowds at Fir Park were growing week by week and at the end of the season they had averaged 8,500. This was largely due to the more attractive style of play which the club adopted with the influx of new players of the calibre of Cooper and Burley.

In the 1989 Skol Cup, Motherwell ousted Kilmarnock from the tournament at Rugby Park by a scoreline of 4–1. The goals were scored by Nicky Cusack (two), Stevie Kirk and Jamie Dolan. A goal from Paul Kinnaird, which was actually his very first senior goal in Scottish football, was enough to end Motherwell's interest in the Skol Cup when St Mirren beat them 1–0 at Paisley.

The Scottish Cup saw Motherwell really rub it into Clyde by 7–0 at Fir Park in their third round contest. Our goals came from McCart, Cooper (penalty), Arnott, Russell, Bryce, Kirk and

*(Left to right): George Burley, Nick Cusack and Paul McLean,
Motherwell's new signings for 1989/90*

Gahagan. This built up a lot of confidence and a big support
travelled to Tynecastle for the fourth round. Motherwell went
down by 4—0, their heaviest defeat for four years. Strangely enough,
this was just another in a string of defeats which Motherwell
suffered at the hands of 'Doddie' McDonald's team in season 1989/
90. In all, Hearts recorded five victories over us in that season.

1990/91

Tommy McLean really splashed out at the start of season 1990/
91. He bought Luc Nijholt from a Swiss team and the Dutch
player settled very quickly. Ian Angus was yet another buy and
Joe McLeod also was signed from Tommy's brother's team at
Tannadice. Iain Ferguson was purchased at the second attempt
and the squad quickly set about blending into a cohesive force.

After beating Morton 4—3 in the Skol Cup the team went down
by 2—0 to Dundee United. Favourable away results proved to be
difficult to come by for some strange reason because the team
were playing with authority at home.

George Burley moved to Ayr United as player/manager and Jim Griffin and John Philliben were in contention for the number two jersey until Luc Nijholt returned from a spell out of the team with a broken leg and staked his claim for the position.

On Saturday, 23 November, Tommy McLean introduced Phil O'Donnell to the squad, one of the best players ever produced at Fir Park, and he played very creditably at left back against McDowell of St Mirren. Motherwell managed a 1–1 draw on that day. Phil's next game was against Rangers at Ibrox on 16 February 1991.

Dougie Arnott started scoring goals and at the turn of the year there was a feeling in the club that something was working well. A unique atmosphere prevailed.

In the dressing-room, spirits were high and after the third round victory in the Scottish Cup at Aberdeen the whole euphoric feeling seemed to grow greater week by week. By the time that Falkirk, Morton and then Celtic had been disposed of, the certainty that 'Motherwell's name is on the Cup' seemed to take over. The rest is history. Motherwell triumphed by 4–3 over Dundee United in extra time and the whole community went bananas!

Even four weeks later, as these notes are penned, the all-pervading feeling of triumphant jubilation still prevails.

We as a club put our destiny in the hands of Tommy McLean and he has guided us, at times with a degree of trepidation, for the past seven years. He took a fading club and gave it belief in itself.

Everyone's job will be just that little bit easier now. Bobby Jenks is now able to attract better youngsters because they see what young Phil O'Donnell achieved. On the commercial side we now have a new sponsor for the team. Motorola will be taking over from the Ian Skelly Group who have had a most harmonious relationship with the football club for the past seven years. Ian Skelly Ltd will continue to have an honoured and esteemed presence at Fir Park. As befits an association which has built up a great relationship over the years, this will prevail for years to come.

Motorola are a worldwide organisation with a manufacturing complex in East Kilbride. They were impressed by the community response to Motherwell's Cup achievements and they decided to become involved in football for the first time in the history of their company. They look upon this as a way to put something

Stevie Kirk and Iain Ferguson with Phil O'Donnell. Young Phil made his first-team debut on Saturday 23 November 1990

back into the local community which is suffering from the ravages of closures and cut-backs. As a result, Motherwell Football Club will benefit from the backing of one of the best companies operating in the United Kingdom.

A press release issued by Motherwell on 13 June 1991 announced the sponsorship switch:

> Motherwell Football Club are pleased to announce that their major sponsors for season 1991/92 will be MOTOROLA. This East Kilbride-based company is part of an international organisation which is ranked as one of the leading manufacturers of microchips in the world.
>
> This breaks new ground for MOTOROLA who have never before been involved in soccer sponsorship and we at Motherwell Football Club feel very honoured indeed that we project the type of image within the community with which MOTOROLA are happy to be associated.

(Left to right): John Swinburne, Davie Cooper, Dr George Bennet (MD of Motorola), Alan Dick, Colin O'Neill, John Chapman, Tony Joyce (Director of External Affairs for Motorola), Joe McLeod and Bill Dickie

As a major employer within Lanarkshire, MOTOROLA are keen to be involved within the community and indirectly their input will be reflected upon the employment situation locally as Motherwell Football Club undertake the substantial major ground improvements which are required by the Taylor Report. At this point we can confirm that this will be a one year agreement with a further year's option.

We are grateful to the Ian Skelly Group for the sponsorship and support which they have given us over the past seven years and we will maintain an honourable association with them for many years to come.

Both Dr George Bennett, Managing Director of Motorola, and Mr Tony Joyce, their Director of External Affairs, were at Fir Park representing their company, and although the launch was a 'low key' affair a good understanding existed between both sets of officials by the end of the day. This augurs well for a long-standing relationship.

Chapter Seven

A FUNNY THING HAPPENED ON THE WAY TO HAMPDEN

The Vice-Presidents Club at Fir Park is located in the Centenary Suite underneath the main stand. The membership is made up of businessmen, managers, self-employed people, retired executives and ordinary fans who have one thing in common: they are Motherwell fanatics and they also enjoy the creature comforts available to them as members of the VP Club. It is a very civilised way to support your team, with the plush surroundings, the bar facilities, pre-match meals if required, half-time snacks and free programmes.

When the draw was known for the third round of the Cup, Peter Callan, the club president, phoned in and suggested that we run a bus, and so for the first Cup match of the season a coach was organised for Aberdeen. Lunch was booked at the Skean Dhu Hotel and a block of tickets ordered from Aberdeen for their main stand.

After a very enjoyable run to the Granite City and an excellent meal there was time for refreshments and relaxation before moving to Pittodrie. In the car park of the hotel we picked up Craig Brown, who was about to call a taxi, and gave him a lift to the match.

Being well organised, the VP Club had obtained a pass into the Dons car park which is just across the road from the grandstand. The members duly alighted and made their way to the match.

Charlie Mulholland, a well-kent figure in the club, found himself seated beside a group of Aberdeen fans and throughout the game they exchanged pleasantries and applauded each other's team when the occasion warranted.

Stevie Kirk, of course, scored with his blistering shot after only 18 seconds on the park and won the game for Motherwell. When the final whistle blew, Charlie Mulholland, never one to rub anyone's nose in it, turned to the group of Aberdeen fans and said, 'Well, I hope you go on and at least win the League.'

He was shaken rigid by the venomous reply of a well-dressed middle-aged lady in the group when she snarled: 'I only hope that Ravenscraig shuts on Monday!'

Charlie was really taken aback and shook his head sadly as he made his way to the car park. 'Some people really take their football too seriously,' he stated as he told the above yarn to those within earshot.

At the end of the game there was a minor exchange of pungent opinions in another area of the stand and the ones to blame were a few upset Aberdonians. A senior police officer put in an instant appearance and the situation quietened down. Along with another senior colleague he followed the 'Well fans right up to the VP Club coach. Entering the vehicle, he asked who was in charge of this group and I admitted liability.

'This bus has no right to be in this car park,' he stated.

'You really take defeat very hard indeed, officer,' I responded.

His face flushed up and he started blaming some of our party for the mini-flare-up of shouting at the end of the game. David Lindsay was angered by this and there was a heated exchange between the two officers of the law and David.

'I thought that the problem people may have been on that other bus,' said the man in blue, indicating the East Kilbride mini-bus, 'but I have checked them out and their behaviour is impeccable.'

'My God,' I thought to myself, 'there is no answer to that!'

'I will see to it that this bus is banned from this car park in future,' the officer said and even though it was pointed out to him that on arrival we had the Scotland assistant manager aboard, he remained adamant.

So there you are, Craig Brown. The next time you go to Pittodrie you may have to park away over at the beach because the law might bar you from the car park if you are in the VP coach.

There was only one coach at the Aberdeen game. By the time

Jim Bett v Bobby Russell in a Motherwell v Aberdeen match at Fir Park

we reached the final this had risen to 12 VP Club coaches with every seat filled.

By the way, I hope that I haven't given the impression that there is anything untoward in the conduct of the East Kilbride Branch of 'Well supporters because nothing could be farther from the truth. Having had the pleasure of travelling all over the country with them I can vouch for their sense of loyalty and also for their own pawky sense of humour.

It was while on our way to an Aberdeen game a few years ago that they spotted that gem of a sign which bore the legend: 'Keep Grampian Beautiful'. Some wit had written underneath this sign: 'Sell Davie Dodds'. I would suspect that this addition to the sign was added on by a supporter of Rangers who had been playing at Aberdeen the previous week.

We always take the coast road up to Aberdeen and return by the same route. At a recent AGM of the East Kilbride Branch, one of the members asked, 'Mr Chairman, would it be possible to come back from Aberdeen a different way this season?'

Quick as a flash the chairman, Martin Rose, enquired, 'Do you mean that you want to come home SOBER?'

At one time the East Kilbride Branch ran as many as two double-decker buses to matches but in recent years they have been reduced to a mini-bus. It is confidently expected that with the recent success of the team they will return to travelling in luxury coaches.

Stevie Kirk, who started our Cup run at Aberdeen when he scored that unforgettable goal after only 18 seconds on the field

Chapter Eight

ON OUR WAY

To see a whole community seize upon an opportunity to shake off the drab, depressive, desolate images of everyday life and reality in an area which has been systematically deprived of its fundamental identity is an unnerving experience.

The steel industry has been at the heart of Motherwell for generations. Through its smoke and grime, allied to the sweat and expertise of its workforce, it afforded a solid base upon which the town prospered. The town was inexorably linked to steel.

Suddenly, distant accountants, economists and politicians decided to bring this association to an end. All that is left now is a mere fraction of a once great and thriving industry and that fraction is constantly fighting a dour rearguard action against the overwhelming forces of bureaucracy and the balance sheet.

The only relief from this oppressive run-down of the community's life source came from Motherwell Football Club's inspiring Scottish Cup run. The bleakness of the economic situation not only encouraged the players and management team to succeed, it actually DEMANDED success. Failure was unthinkable and untenable. All those people in the Lanarkshire area had experienced the bitter taste of defeat in their everyday lives and here at last was an opportunity for them to savour success. Nothing else but outright victory would satisfy them.

In some strange way this tremendous resolve to succeed managed to percolate through to every player in the team. They constantly commented in interviews that 'we must do our best for

Some of the Motherwell fans both old and new

Some 'Well fans in full regalia

the fans and the community'. The hundreds of schoolkids who cheered the team bus away as the players headed for Irvine to prepare for the big day underlined just exactly what was at stake not only for Motherwell, the team, but also for Motherwell, the town.

To be fair to the players, they shouldered the burden placed upon them and lived up to their traditional name of 'The Steelmen'. They played with courage, skill and resolve, determined to win not only for themselves but for a whole community which had rallied round them and turned out in their tens of thousands at Hampden to support them.

In the lead up to the final I confided to some friends that I was actually worried for some of 'the new fans' who had recently turned out to support the 'Well. While we – 'the hard core' – would be able to face any result in the final and continue to support the team, I feared for these more recent converts who were wearing their claret and amber hearts on their sleeves. The backlash could well have been unpleasant but one thing is certain, defeat could have abruptly ended allegiance to the team from a whole host of new supporters.

The freshness of this new support was very uplifting and exhilarating. They proudly wore the claret and amber colours of their team and they were far more vociferous than those who had been regulars for many years. It wasn't the new brigade that sat with bowed heads during the interval before extra time got underway. Neither was it the new brigade who simply couldn't bear to watch the drama unfold after Stevie Kirk had scored Motherwell's fourth goal. They – the new brigade – remained confident and continued to sing and cheer their team on to their finest victory.

I underestimated them and I take my hat off to them – like the team, they too were superb.

The masses who turned out to pay homage to their heroes on the Sunday enjoyed their moments of glory and victory, as a community. THEY THOROUGHLY DESERVED IT!!

After the victory in the replay against Celtic the whole town of Motherwell went mad. Shops started to decorate their windows with claret and amber. Banks kitted their tellers in Motherwell tops. Schools ran competitions to design the best greeting card for the local team.

The local Council organised a competition to find the best decorated shop. Wilson Humphries and the Provost were the adjudicators. Bunting appeared overnight and huge banners with 'C'MON THE WELL' were put up at all the approaches to the town.

Bus companies did a roaring trade and three weeks before the final there wasn't a bus available for hire in the West of Scotland. Buses were contracted to take groups to Hampden and they were hired from as far afield as Carlisle and North Berwick. Some companies were ripping off groups by charging £150 for a bus hire to Hampden.

On the morning that tickets were put on sale about £50,000 worth were sold before lunchtime. Some fans slept overnight in their cars in order to obtain stand tickets.

The queue at 8.00 a.m. stretched right round into the grounds of the school at the end of Firpark Street. Anyone attempting to park their car found themselves beyond the Glencairn Laundry area. By 11.00 a.m. the whole of Section 'J' had been sold and supporters patiently waited the return of Andy Russell who had been sent into the SFA at Park Gardens for a further allocation. The offices of the SFA had been closed for the Bank Holiday but Bill Dickie managed to contact Jim Farry and more precious tickets were made available to Motherwell.

Naturally, demands for stand tickets greatly exceeded the allocation received. Requests flooded into Fir Park for pre-match meals and in order to meet the demand a marquee was ordered to seat 300 fans. Ian Skelly sponsored this marquee which took up half the penalty area at the south end of the park. Over 500 were catered for with pre-match lunches; Elanjay, the official caterers to Motherwell FC, excelled themselves and Lynette Boyle organised everything in her usual competent manner. Bottles of 'Motherwell' labelled wine were snapped up and they were sold as quickly as they could be opened.

The carnival atmosphere was heightened by the 'face-painters' who were on duty in the town centre. All sorts of fancy dress costumes were on view.

Fans from the Orb in Bellshill hired a huge Rolls Royce limousine. This luxury vehicle was given the red-carpet treatment by the police and was ushered right up to the main entrance of Hampden. The mounted police kept the crowds back as the chauffeur opened the doors. Much to their surprise happy punters all resplendent in their Motherwell jerseys and jeans decanted!

The great good humour of the crowds at Hampden had to be seen to be appreciated. Dundee United and 'Well fans mingled happily. Family groups were strongly in evidence and this made a most pleasant change from all the sectarian bitterness which is associated with cup matches involving the 'Old Firm'.

Edward Street was decorated with bunting supplied by Ian Adams and put up by John Brogan, who sent round one of his 'Cherrypickers' to do the job.

A 'Win or Lose' party was organised by the leisure department of Motherwell District Council. This was to be held in the Civic Centre. Those who bought tickets were confident that it would be a 'Win' party.

Confidence in the town was running at an all-time high and everyone you spoke to seemed to make the same statement – that they were certain 'Motherwell's name is on the Cup this time'.

In the build-up to the final, the normal routine at Motherwell carried on as usual as far as training was concerned. Outwith training hours there was a constant stream of newspaper reporters and photographers plus television and radio teams vying with one another to find a story which was a bit offbeat and out of the ordinary.

The *Daily Record* made contact with the seven survivors of the 1952 Cup Final and organised a photo-session and lunch at Hampden about a week or so before the final. Craig Halkett made the contacts and Rodger Baillie did the interviews. The task of getting the 1952 players together was made much easier due to the fact that Motherwell have a quite unique Former Players Club. There is a nominal membership fee and four times each season they meet and have a pre-match meal and then watch the match and have another exchange of views and pleasantries before heading for home.

There are players from the 1940s right through to the 1980s, including such favourites from the past as the Ancell Babes, the Cup winning survivors, the 1965 Summer Cup winners plus the players from more recent times.

To my knowledge this is the only Former Players Club in the country. The members meet in the Vice-Presidents Club at

The 1952 Cup winners

Motherwell and their organisation is sponsored by Mr Ian Skelly. When these stars from the past congregate, the games which they recall and the yarns which they spin bring all those games of yesteryear back to life.

To return to the *Daily Record* and their session with the 1952 team. Willie Kilmarnock was in attendance and Jimmy Watson hadn't seen him for decades. The 'old-timers' were given claret and amber jerseys, scarves and tammies and out they went to the centre-circle with the Scottish Cup. Craig Halkett took a series of pictures which would be laid aside and used in the final run-up to the big day at Hampden.

Rodger Baillie presided over the lunch and he took copious notes for his article. He was surprised to learn, for example, that over 250,000 fans watched the semi-final games between Motherwell and Hearts and that 136,304 fans were in attendance at the final game against Dundee in 1952.

The survivors spoke highly of Johnny Johnstone, Archie Shaw, Willie Redpath and Johnny Aitkenhead who had all passed on.

Present at the lunch were Willie Kilmarnock, Charlie Cox, Andy Paton, Tommy Sloan, Wilson Humphries, Archie Kelly and Jimmy Watson.

When asked what memory they had about that great day 39 years ago when they beat Dundee 4–0, Charlie Cox and Tommy Sloan both said it was the awesome 'wall of sound' that met them as they walked out on to the park. Archie Kelly pointed out that this didn't affect the rest of the team because they had all experienced the same sensation in the 1951 Cup Final the year before when Celtic won by the only goal of the game, scored by big John McPhail.

It was generally agreed that the modern game is faster, although Jimmy Watson argued that if they had been able to play in lightweight boots and light jerseys and use the modern ball which doesn't get heavier on a wet day as the game goes on, the older players would definitely have been able to hold their own if they were playing today.

Andy Paton emphatically declared that he was convinced that Motherwell were a certainty to win the Cup this year because Tommy McLean's team had the same attributes as the 1952 squad. They were prepared to battle, fight and play for each other.

Another yarn, this time by Jimmy Watson, was received with great guffaws of laughter. Jimmy recounted that in a game against Rangers in 1951 at Fir Park, Sammy Cox clashed with him and swore at him. Charlie Faultless was the referee and Jimmy went up to him and complained, 'Hey ref, Sammy Cox just called me a Fenian "B".'

'How do you know that he was talking to you?' he enquired.

'Because I'm the only Fenian "B" on the park,' Jimmy replied with a laugh.

Willie Kilmarnock has fond memories of that 1952 Cup final. He saved the day on three occasions in the first half when he cleared the ball off the goal line with Johnny Johnstone beaten. Willie's main pastime nowadays is bowls, a game which he really enjoys.

Charlie Cox is still the perfect gentleman that he always was — even on the park. He had one of the hardest jobs on that day 39 years ago. He had to mark Billy Steele, the perfect 'inside forward', and it was mainly due to Charlie's close marking that Billy had a very ineffective game.

Andy Paton had a hot handful in Bobby Flavell, a real live-wire of a centre forward. He was blotted out of the game and Andy even found the time to back up his forwards in the second half.

Tommy Sloan was a real flying machine. When he got possession and touched the ball past the opposing full back, nobody could catch him. His fast raiding was a constant source of worry to the Dundee defence and with a bit of luck he could have been on the scoresheet to make that scoreline 5–0.

Wilson Humphries was the workhorse of the front five. He was fast and very strong and in many ways he could be compared to the great Willie Waddell, especially when he was played wide on the right wing. He possessed a lethal shot and was always a prolific scorer.

Archie Kelly was my ideal striker, or centre forward as they were known then. Brave, fast, elusive, quick on the turn plus an instinctive ability to score goals. Good in the air or on the ground. I remember his first game for Motherwell against Rangers. He turned and left Willie Woodburn stranded and then shot from 30 yards and beat Bobby Brown all ends up. A *great* striker and he must have been a pleasure to play alongside.

Jimmy Watson was an elegant player with tremendous natural ability. He was the complete inside forward and the way that he could link up with Johnny Aitkenhead was uncanny. He scored a high percentage of his goals with his head but he also had a ferocious shot, particularly in his right foot.

That gives the old stagers a wee mention – very well deserved at that!

I gave the 1952 players a colour photograph of the '52 team and this was well received since this was the first colour picture of their team that they had actually seen.

The seven heroes from the past were guests of honour at Fir Park on the day of the final, and as Wilson Humphries stated, 'This is great. I'm a better player today than I ever was and it is great to feel that our performances all those years ago will never be forgotten.'

Wilson, I can assure you that that is certainly the case, and now the same will apply to the 1991 squad.

During Wilson's speech at the Civic Reception after the Cup victory he was addressing the younger 'Well players and he told the following story.

'George Best went to buy a newspaper one day and he saw that the vendor was clad in the light blue of Manchester City. He decided to wind the vendor up and after purchasing the paper he enquired of him what the best way was to get to Maine Road? Instantly recognising George Best the vendor, quick as a flash replied, "George – PRACTICE, PRACTICE AND MORE PRACTICE."'

Over and above the seven 1952 Cup-winning players who were at the final I spotted John Martis, Sammy and Billy Reid, Jackie Hunter, Alan MacKay, Matt Thomson, Willie McCallum, Willie Hunter, Andy Weir, Ian St John, Pat Quinn, John Goldthorpe, Willie Barclay, Dixie Deans, Willie McSeveney, Peter Millar, Davy Whiteford and Bobby Graham.

It is great to see this loyal support from former players. I have no doubt that there were many others at the Cup final – I only listed those players that I actually saw on the big day.

It was well named the 'Family Final' and it has set a standard of behaviour for the future. To survive, football must attract families to matches, and displays such as that served up by both Dundee United and Motherwell will go a long way to establishing our football back where it should be once again.

A family game, enjoyed by families – that must continue to be our aim.

As the media descended upon Fir Park, publicity was accorded to many of the backroom and support staff.

Andy Russell, complete with huge cigar, became a bit of a cult figure. The groundsman in one memorable TV interview stated: 'Jim McLean might as well save himself the toll fee at the Forth Road Bridge because he has no chance of winning.'

Lucy Scott was another who was interviewed in depth, as was Alison Douse, the young YTS girl in the office. No stone was left unturned as the media tried hard for a new angle or a new face.

Hazel Irvine and Chick Young became near fixtures at the ground. The marquee which was sponsored by Ian Skelly attracted a great deal of attention and the 300 fans who were wined and dined there prior to the game were filmed. Where there was a story, such as the two fans over from California, an interview duly took place.

A few short hours later the whole of Andy Russell's precious

The fans celebrate on Andy Russell's park

grass park was covered by thousands of chanting, cheering fans, saluting the 1991 Cup winners as his forecast came to pass.

In recent years we members of the backroom staff have found ourselves more or less finished, as far as having any chance of picking up honours is concerned, by about the end of April. This season it was completely different. The whole level of activity continued and in fact increased tenfold as the Cup final drew ever nearer.

Ticket allocation was a problem as Alan Dick attempted to spread our meagre supply as fairly as possible. It was a classic case of trying to get a quart (or rather a gallon) into a pint pot.

Karen Murray, who organises the souvenir shop, simply couldn't keep pace with the unprecedented demand for scarves, caps, ties or anything which would serve to announce to the world that the wearer was without question a supporter of Motherwell Football Club.

Margaret MacFarlane had the unenviable task of co-ordinating the arrangements for meals in the club's Centenary Suite and also the Ian Skelly marquee which would take the 300 overspill.

It was a case of everyone pulling together and getting the job done. At Fir Park there is nothing unusual about this because that is exactly what happens behind the scenes all the time. Dedication is as good a word as any to describe the attitude of the backroom staff and it all contributes to a first-class working environment for everyone at the club.

The backroom staff have had rather a good season from a financial point of view. It started away back in July 1990. A second dividend and a whole string of minor dividends brought a nice little cheque for £11,600 from the Australian pools to be shared between Karen, Lucy, Margaret, Andy Russell, Big Tam, Wee Tam and yours truly. When the draw was made for the Scottish Cup and we were paired with Aberdeen, I asked Karen to put my annual flutter on Motherwell to win the Cup. I even managed to coax both her and Mags to add two quid to my tenner. The odds were 66 to 1, which was a lot better than the 14 to 1 which I got away back in 1952. On that occasion I could only afford to risk ten shillings (50p).

After our 4–3 victory, I went to the bookies and a kind gentleman gave me over a thousand pounds for our little betting slip. Not being a regular gambler, I don't expect to be back inside another betting shop until the draw is known for next year's Scottish Cup. Well, at least it is more exciting than buying Electricity Shares . . .

The superstitious acts of players, management and fans alike are wide and varied and often weird and wonderful. They are all totally illogical.

For my own part, after beating Aberdeen in January I carefully noted my attire and made certain that I wore the same suit, shirt, tie, shoes and socks for the next round of the Cup against Falkirk. I brushed this stupid superstition aside for the Morton game but when we only drew I reverted to the 'Aberdeen gear' for the replay. Naturally, I was by now convinced and kept the 'lucky gear' for the semi-final and the replay. It seemed to work again so there was no way that I was going to alter anything for the final.

Tommy McLean always takes his 'lucky tartan blanket' into the dugout. Although I don't recall seeing it at the final, I have no doubt it would be there.

Big Tam Forsyth and Tommy McLean both received a 'lucky

white heather' buttonhole before the matches with Celtic and again wore them 'for good luck' in the final.

No doubt there were 'lucky scarves' and hats galore at Hampden but the most important good luck mascot of all was 'Super Sub' Stevie Kirk. As long as HE was in the pool, 'Well fans felt certain that they simply couldn't lose! Stevie was and always will be everyone's Scottish Cup lucky charm after that tremendous 1991 Cup run.

Mind you, the more logical amongst us will say that superstitions are stupid and without foundation. They are probably right but I have MY Cup gear cleaned and laid aside for next season. I KNOW that it will make no difference to the outcome of any game but who am I to tempt providence?

Good luck messages flooded into Fir Park before the final from every corner of the world. Expatriate Motherwell fans sent their best wishes and words of encouragement.

The one which I thought was straight from the heart came from Johnny Gahagan, who actually came very close to putting Motherwell out of the Cup when he scored Morton's equaliser at Cappielow to take that match to a nerve wracking penalty shootout. Here is John's letter to the team:

JOHN GAHAGAN
MORTON FC

TO MOTHERWELL FC

A wee prayer that Saturday the 18 May 1991 will go down in the history books as one of the greatest in the town's footballing lifetime. My best wishes to all the men who pull on a claret and amber jersey on Final Day, and thoughts also to the unfortunate lads who, for one reason or another, will have to miss out. May the match be memorable, the celebrations long lasting and the Motherwell medals be GOLD.

May I take this opportunity to sincerely thank everyone at Fir Park from chairman, directors, management, players, ground staff and supporters for 11 magnificent years culminating in an incredible testimonial year. I will be eternally grateful to you all, and the memories will stay with me to my dying days.

PS I'm not half jealous at you lot getting to the final without me. GOOD LUCK!

JOHN GAHAGAN

Chapter Nine

'WELL'S CUP FINALISTS

ALLY MAXWELL

For raw courage, Alastair Maxwell's performance in the Scottish Cup final has no equal.

He was at full stretch for a high ball when John Clark collided with him in mid-air. I reckon that it must have been John's hip which did the damage to Maxie's spleen and stomach muscles. Ally collapsed in a heap and much to the surprise of most at the match that day, referee David Syme didn't even award a free kick. The ball ran out for a shy and Motherwell's physio, Bobby Holmes, rushed on to the park to assess the damage to the prostrate goalkeeper.

Bobby quickly ascertained that there were no broken or cracked ribs and Ally eventually struggled to his feet. All the time he was clutching his left side.

The match got underway but it soon became apparent that Ally was really struggling, a fact underlined shortly after his injury when a long range shot from Dundee United's Dave Bowman squeezed home at the far post to give United an equaliser. Under normal circumstances Alastair Maxwell would have toyed with an attempt at goal of this nature.

Goals by Phil O'Donnell and Ian Angus took a great deal of strain off the hard-pressed Motherwell defenders who had regrouped to give Maxie as much protection as possible. Despite this they were unable to prevent Dundee United from snatching their second goal, a superb header from John O'Neil which would

Ally Maxwell

undoubtedly have found the net even if Maxie hadn't been hampered by injury.

Wave after wave of United attacks continued to founder on the solid 'Well defence, and Maxie was obviously in extreme pain every time he fielded the ball. Tommy Boyd took the bye-kicks.

It was 20 seconds into injury time at the end of 90 minutes when Alan Main thumped yet another tremendous high ball deep into the heart of the Motherwell defence. Darren Jackson met the ball on the first bounce and cleanly headed it past the despairing, diving Alastair Maxwell. It finished up in the net and United were back in the game once more. The score stood at 3–3 and many 'Well fans openly wept. They felt that victory had been snatched from their grasp.

The team gathered round Tommy McLean and Tam Forsyth during the brief interval before extra time got underway. Doctor Logan and Bobby Holmes worked on Alastair Maxwell and Tommy McLean was seriously contemplating putting Stevie Kirk into goal for the last half hour of play. 'I'll be alright, Boss,' Ally assured his manager. 'Let's go and win this,' he said as he struggled to his feet.

The rest is now history. Stevie Kirk scored in the 95th minute and Motherwell valiantly held on . . .

There were three minutes left to play and in yet another blistering attack by Dundee United the ball broke to Maurice

Malpas. He took it in his stride and sent in a screamer of a shot. It was raging into the net, high to the goalie's right, when there was a blue blur. Maxie had thrown himself horizontally and miraculously he managed, somehow, to get a hand to Maurice's shot and deflect the ball over the bar.

Hampden erupted. Everyone knew at that moment there was no way Motherwell would be beaten. A few minutes later and it was all over.

On the Monday after the final, an article by Alan Davidson in the *Evening Times* praised Motherwell's win: 'likewise, their ultimate triumph was totally deserved if only for the seemingly bottomless well of desire and raw courage they showed'. While this obviously refers to the whole team, it is about Alastair Maxwell first and foremost. Near to collapse after the game, Maxie was rushed to the Victoria Infirmary where a lacerated spleen was diagnosed as well as severe internal bruising.

Eight days after the final, I visited Alastair in the Victoria Infirmary. Although he had signed himself out on the Sunday after the final in order to travel on the open-topped bus and pay tribute to all the 'Well fans, he had come close to needing major surgery. However, the word was that he should be home in a day or two and that his injury should self-rectify.

He was voted Player of the Year by the City of Glasgow Friendly Society in conjunction with the *Motherwell Times*. For this he received a Volkswagen Jetta for a year. He was also voted Player of the Year by the Association of Motherwell Supporters Clubs.

Alastair Maxwell was signed by Davie Hay in November 1981 from the Fir Park Boys' Club. His father Ian had introduced him to football at a very early age and Ally and his brother were taken regularly to Fir Park. It was with great pride therefore that Ian saw his son signing professional forms for Motherwell and it was with even greater pride that he saw him holding the Scottish Cup aloft at the end of the greatest Cup final in living memory.

Alastair didn't have an easy time before he finally established himself as Motherwell's number one goalkeeper. He had to challenge others such as Hughie Sproat, Nicky Walker, John Gardiner and Cammy Duncan for the keeper's jersey.

Over 120 games in a row is his proud boast and he is now pushing for that Scotland number one spot. Andy Roxburgh has recognised his potential and included him in his squads and it can only be a matter of time before Alastair Maxwell is chosen as Scotland's top goalkeeper. One thing is certain: his exceptionally brave display in the 1991 Cup final only served to underline what an outstanding prospect he has become.

LUC NIJHOLT

What a season it turned out to be for Luc Nijholt. The Dutchman was signed from BSC Old Boys of Basle at the beginning of August 1990. He quickly settled into Tommy McLean's set-up and he played both at the back and in midfield.

On 25 November 1990 he suffered a nasty leg-break at Parkhead but made his come-back against Celtic at Fir Park on 30 January 1991. As soon as he had fully recaptured his match fitness he again established himself in the team and he played in every game from 2 March against Hearts right through to the end of the season.

A great favourite with the fans, Luc has that continental blend of skill and hardness in the tackle which has added another dimension to Motherwell's performances. He has also offered Tommy McLean a series of options due to his versatility.

Despite the fact that he had missed out on a fair number of games he managed to amass a higher number of performance points than any of his team-mates and he won the Ian Skelly Player of the Year Award for which he received the use of a Volkswagen Jetta for a year.

I asked him how he compared Scottish football with soccer in Holland or Switzerland. 'Scottish football is very quick and very hard but this seems to suit my style of play. I prefer playing here. I did not enjoy Swiss football because nobody seems to really care. In Scotland there is a great passion for the game. I enjoyed the Cup final with the huge crowd and now to win a motor car is tremendous.'

Luc was the only player to receive a yellow card in the final, after a clash with young McKinlay of Dundee United. This was unfortunate because he is essentially a very fair player. He thought that Maxie had shown great courage to continue playing as he did.

69

Luc Nijholt

Another thing that impressed him was the huge turn-out of fans on the Sunday when the team paraded the Cup through Mother-well and Wishaw in an open-topped bus. 'This was definitely the best season of my life,' he stated with an engaging smile.

He is under contract for another two seasons and he has proved to be one of the best acquisitions made by Tommy McLean. He has become an integral part of the Motherwell set-up. The importance of his signing can be assessed by the fact that the Scottish Cup is now back in the boardroom at Fir Park after an absence of 39 years.

Luc Nijholt stood in for the hospitalised Ally Maxwell at the annual presentation of the Supporters' Player of the Year. He gave an excellent account of himself with a well-rehearsed speech which was both humorous and sincere. 'There are three great things in Maxie's life this year,' Luc said. 'Firstly, his first-born child, secondly his call-up to the Scotland squad where he wishes to be number one and thirdly his Scottish Cup medal.

'Maxie has taught me many things since I came to Scotland,' he continued, 'including how to bet on slow horses – but seriously, he has been a good friend to my family and helped me to settle in Scotland.'

Luc Nijholt will be an even better player in season 1991/92 after the experience which he has picked up in his first and highly successful spell in Scottish football. Any youngster could learn quickly by watching Luc. He shows that he is very comfortable on the ball and a master of his chosen profession.

When Luc went to Ian Skelly's to pick up his car he told me that the local newspaper in his hometown in Holland carried the headline in the sports pages: 'LUC WINS SCOTTISH CUP MEDAL AND MOTOR CAR'.

As the players were lining up to be introduced before the match Luc spotted me in the grandstand and I impersonated somebody steering a car with an imaginary steering wheel and then gave him the thumbs-up sign. This was a wee private joke between us because I had been telling him earlier in the week that he was leading the league table for the Ian Skelly Player of the Year Award. 'All you need to do is go out and have a great game and you will win a motor car,' I told him. Luc laughed and gave a wave and then made out as though he was steering an imaginary car. He certainly looked to be one of the coolest players in our team.

His sharp interventions were the cause of many United attacks breaking down as he set about his duties in his usual uncompromising way. For Luc, a Hampden Cup final was business as usual.

TOMMY BOYD

Tommy Boyd arrived at Fir Park during Jock Wallace's term in office as manager. His assistant, Frank Connor, was instrumental in signing Tom.

As it turned out, this 16-year-old YTS footballer was to develop and mature into a top class professional who has been capped for his country. He was also installed as team captain by Tommy McLean in 1985 after Ally Mauchlen and Gary McAllister were transferred to Leicester City. Tom Boyd held this position right up until his final game with the club – the Cup final against Dundee United on Saturday, 18 May 1991, when he had the pleasure of holding the Scottish Cup aloft as he saluted the fans of Motherwell.

How did you feel, Tam, as you actually lifted the trophy? 'It was like a dream come true,' he replied. 'What a way to end my time at Fir Park. When I first came on to the park the pressure was almost overwhelming and the noise was awesome. However, we soon settled once the game got underway and from then on we just tried all we knew and won through in the end.'

Tommy Boyd could have signed for Nottingham Forest and actually played in the FA Cup final against Tottenham Hotspur, but he remained loyal to the Motherwell fans who had taken him to their hearts all those years ago and watched him turn into one of the finest young defenders in the country. Now a Chelsea player, we can at least look forward to watching him playing in Scotland's colours for the foreseeable future.

Efficient and effective in any of the defensive or midfield positions, he gave his finest performances at left back. But it wasn't until the arrival of Davie Cooper at Fir Park that he realised his full potential in this role. A short ball to Davie and then he would go off on the overlap, secure in the knowledge that 'Coop' would flight the ball accurately into his path. About this stage in his career Tommy also started to exhibit a phenomenal turn of speed which devastated defences.

His only goal in the 1991 Scottish Cup campaign came in the replay at Cappielow. He started the move back in his own penalty area and surged forward to meet a clearance from a Morton defender squarely with his brow to score from about 15 yards out.

Tommy won a motor car last season when he came out on top for the Ian Skelly Player of the Year Award. In his first season in the first team he also won a motor car from Trust Motors. He was only 17 at the time and hadn't passed his driving test. Trust Motors did put him through his test but it was quite some time before he lived down all those daft pictures which showed him on a bike with L-plates prominently displayed.

For a while it looked as though Tommy might even miss the Cup final due to a nasty injury which he picked up in the semi-final replay against Celtic. He missed out on five games and this was his longest spell out of the first team apart from the time when he broke a bone in his foot a few seasons ago.

One thing is certain: If Tom Boyd is ever asked in the future what was the best game he ever played in, he will answer unhesitatingly: 'The final of the Scottish Cup 1991.'

Motherwell fans everywhere will wish Tommy Boyd well in his

Tommy Boyd

football career in the future. He will rank with the all-time Motherwell greats and as captain of the '91 Cup winners he is now a legend.

I always felt that I contributed just a little to Tommy Boyd's career. Back in 1983 I took a phone call from Ross Mathie, the SFA coach in charge of the Youth team at that time. 'Could I speak to Jock Wallace?' he enquired.

'Jock's out at training,' I replied.

'It's Ross Mathie here, John. Scotland Under-18s are playing a trial game at Greenock tomorrow and we have had a couple of call-offs. I'm looking for a forward and a defender and I wondered if Big Jock had anyone through there who could help out?'

'Well, Ross, there are a couple of youngsters here who wouldn't let you down – Paul McFadden who is a striker and Tam Boyd who is a sweeper – and I'm quite sure that the manager would help you out.'

Jock Wallace readily agreed and the two lads were duly sent off to Greenock. They both did well and were included in Scotland's next Under-18 squad. Young Paul only played in the first half of the game but Tommy Boyd went from strength to strength and won a series of Under-18 and Under-21 caps before graduating to play for Scotland where he had a memorable debut and 'made' the winning goal.

Although Tommy is a natural right-side player he has adapted well to the left back position and he is very comfortable with both feet. He has always worked very hard at improving his game. He has come a long way since his early YTS days. He can be proud of the fact that he was the very first YTS trainee footballer who seized his opportunity, became established in the Motherwell first team and then won full international honours.

The YTS scheme has been maligned in many quarters but when you consider that Tom Boyd, Chris McCart, Jim Griffin and Phil O'Donnell all worked their way through the YTS ranks to star in the 1991 Scottish Cup final, then you will agree that the YTS scheme has been of immense benefit to these players and to Motherwell fans alike.

About five weeks after the final I had a surprise visitor during my lunch break when Tommy Boyd dropped in for a chat. I congratulated him on his move to Chelsea for the all-time Motherwell record fee of £800,000.

Tom Boyd hurdles over Richard Gough during a Motherwell v Rangers clash

Tom Boyd chases John Clark, with Bowman and Kirk in the background

'How are you settling in, Tam?' I asked.

'It's great, John,' he replied. 'Everyone has been very helpful. My wife and I are now looking around down there for a place to stay and it looks as though we could finish up in the Beaconsfield area. This isn't too far from the training ground and it looks like a nice place to settle down.'

'It must have been quite a month for you,' I said.

'Well, John, we won the Cup in a really fantastic game, I signed for Chelsea and of course I got married – all within 11 days – so you could say that May 1991 was quite a month. My big worry was whether or not I was going to be fit enough to play in the final because after that five-game lay-off I only managed three reserve games.

'When the game went into extra time I nearly collapsed at the thought of 30 minutes more to play and I did get a touch of cramp near the end but I suppose that is only to be expected.

'It was with mixed feelings that I lifted the Cup. I was overjoyed but I knew that I had played my last game with the boys and they're a great bunch. I was going to miss out on all those weeks of celebrations and also playing in Europe. But for the long term it was too good an opportunity and I had to take it and move on.

'There are quite a few Scots down at Chelsea and we now have Ian Porterfield as the manager. I am really looking forward to next season.

'I only hope that the fans treat me as well as the Motherwell supporters have done because they were always great to me and I really appreciated their support.'

Again I wished him all the best before he left and he promised, 'I'll be up to see the European games at Fir Park if I can get away.'

JIM GRIFFIN

Jim Griffin was signed by Tommy McLean from the Fir Park Boys' Club in June 1985. He had been dogged by injuries during his earlier years with Motherwell and it has taken him much longer to become established in the first team pool than many would have expected.

'Griff' played the greatest game of his life on Saturday, 18 May 1991, against Dundee United in the Scottish Cup final.

Nobody ever doubted his ability or effort but nearly every time

Jim Griffin

he managed to break through from the reserves to play in the 'big team' he would pick up an injury and have to start all over again. Last season, for example, he only managed six full appearances plus another five as substitute.

Earlier this season he was again settling nicely into the first team when he was assaulted during training by Colin McNair, who was instantly dismissed by Tommy McLean. McNair was later charged by the police. He was eventually found guilty and fined. As Jim Griffin stated after the trial, 'That fine was a joke. I had to pay twice as much in dental fees after my teeth were kicked out while I was lying on the ground.'

Fortunately Jim Griffin fought his way back into the team and he soon proved his worth. A model professional, he was booked for the first time ever this season and although he plays very hard he is always scrupulously fair.

Jim Griffin and Chris McCart are great buddies and this is only natural because there is only three months between them in age.

'Griff' was actually a 'first foot' on 1 January 1967 in the Griffin household.

He is very calm under pressure and he displays good vision allied to tenacious tackling ability. The contest between 'Griff' and Jim McInally was one of the highlights of the whole final and 'Griff' came out on top against his rival who can boast a fair number of Scottish caps. Jim is also a tireless worker in the midfield 'powerhouse area' and that is where the struggle for supremacy was won and lost in the 1991 Cup final.

Now that he has shaken off that persistent injury hoodoo Jim Griffin will go from strength to strength. I would expect him to become an ever-present in 1991/92 because sheer bad luck can only last so long.

Jim is due a break and he got one when he retained his place in the Cup final. Many astute experts rated his performance as being the best on the park while others listed only Phil O'Donnell in front of the ever enthusiastic 'Griff'.

The all-important opening goal in the Cup final was scored by Iain Ferguson when he headed home an inch-perfect cross from 'Griff', but without any shadow of a doubt the most important touch of the ball in Jim Griffin's whole career will be that deflection of John Clark's shot in the 122nd minute of the Cup final. This turned a certain goal into a corner kick and Dundee United hadn't time to take the corner before David Syme blew his whistle for time up. Without Jim's deflection everyone would have been subjected to a traumatic penalty shoot-out. When you consider that 'Maxie' was only playing by memory due to his serious injuries the odds would once again have swung in favour of Dundee United.

Jim Griffin was picked out by Ally McCoist who had given up his customary seat on the subs bench to sit beside Jock Brown and help out with the commentary during the game. In actual fact I was very impressed by Ally's analysis of the game as it ebbed and flowed for the full 120-plus minutes. As I mentioned earlier, he highlighted Jim Griffin's contribution. 'He's a real player's player,' stated Ally as he went on to explain that Jim was the type of footballer who seldom gets the credit which is due to him.

The jousts between 'Griff' and McInally also brought comment from Ally. Neither gave an inch and neither resorted to any underhand tactics. It was simply a robust, strong encounter

Craig Paterson wins this high ball under pressure from John Clark

between two superb professionals and at the end of the day you simply had to give the edge to 'Griff'.

CRAIG PATERSON

Craig Paterson is one of that rare breed of 'second generation' footballers. His father played centre-half behind the famous Hibs five – Smith, Johnstone, Reilly, Turnbull and Ormond. Alfie Conn Junior was another example and in opposition to Craig in the Cup final was Dave Bowman, whose father Andy Bowman played wing-half for Hearts.

Tommy McLean signed the tall defender from Rangers on the last day of 1986 and at £25,000 he proved to be an extremely sound investment. His 6 feet 2½ inches were invaluable in the first half of that epic Cup final when he blotted out young Duncan Ferguson so effectively that he was substituted at half-time.

Craig was team captain of Rangers and he also gained a wealth of experience with Hibs before his £250,000 move to Ibrox. Tommy McLean harnessed Craig's experience and utilised it at the heart of the 'Well defence. Craig was also instrumental in coaching youngsters around him. Young Chris McCart, for example, has turned into one of the finest central defenders in the country, and this is in no small measure due to the influence of Craig Paterson.

Now 31 years of age, Craig brought a solidity to the 'Well back four and he also posed problems for the opposition at set pieces. He scored a fair number of goals since moving to Fir Park and he had innumerable 'assists' to his credit. Injury caused him to miss out on the semi-finals but he proved that he was fit and back to his best in time to get the nod for the final.

In his early days at Motherwell he struck up an outstanding partnership with Tam McAdam, his long time Old Firm rival from Celtic. It was a joy to watch the instinctive understanding which these two quickly built up. Their partnership was instrumental in helping Motherwell through on many occasions during the formative years of Tommy McLean's team.

Craig Paterson is exceptionally commanding in the air and his positional sense and tackling ability made him an invaluable member of the Cup-winning squad.

During his spell at Ibrox, Craig had the reputation for being

Craig Paterson

injury prone. He certainly managed to lose that tag during his four-and-a-half years at Fir Park because during that time he missed only nine games through injury.

Craig is very articulate and his views on football are worth listening to. In my opinion he played the best football of his career after coming to Fir Park and he certainly fulfilled all the early promise of his Easter Road days.

CHRIS McCART

Chris McCart is one of those rare individuals. He is a central defender and despite the fact that he plays at the heart of the 'Well defence where the demands are greatest, he achieved the near impossible task of being an ever-present in season 1990/91. In the previous season he recorded 33 appearances plus one substitute match out of 36 league games.

What makes this unusual? Well, to avoid accumulating ten penalty points is surely a major achievement in the hurly-burly of

81

A young Chris McCart, who has taken over as team captain now that Tom Boyd has left for Chelsea

the Premier League. Chris is scrupulously fair in the tackle and you never see him question any refereeing decisions. I think this is something that is in his make-up although he had a great mentor during his formative years in Tam McAdam, who never ever argued with referees. 'I've played a long time,' Tam once told me, 'and I have yet to see a referee change his mind after a player complains about a decision – so why complain?' Chris McCart has exactly the same approach.

Chris McCart is over six feet in height and very commanding in the air. A big future is forecast for him at international level and Jim McLean chose him in his pool of home-based Scots to play in the Scottish League centenary match at the start of the 1990/91 season.

Now married and staying close to Fir Park, this quiet, unassuming player has recently taken over the captaincy of the club which was vacated by Tommy Boyd when he moved on to Chelsea.

Chris really relished that Cup final victory over Dundee United. 'It was great for the fans, great for the team and great for the community,' he enthused when I asked him just how he felt about that 4–3 result. He was a real stalwart right through the whole 120 minutes and time and again his timely interventions broke up United attacks.

Chris is one of those players who richly deserves all the success which he will undoubtedly attain during his footballing career. He is one of the genuine 'nice guys' in the game. It is great to see a player's talent develop over the years and Chris McCart has certainly lived up to all expectations.

As a youngster of 16 he played a full season in the left back position in the reserve team and although he was so young he never looked out of place. Once he gets his foot in the International door I am certain Andy Roxburgh will find that he will quickly become an indispensable feature of his Scotland team.

Big things lie ahead for this talented defender and he thoroughly deserves all the good things that will come his way.

DOUGIE ARNOTT

If a poll was taken of all central defenders asking them which player they least looked forward to playing against, Dougie Arnott

Dougie Arnott challenges for a high ball

would be one of the front runners for that nomination. I reckon that Ian St John had many similarities with Dougie Arnott. They both buzzed about all over the park with unlimited energy. They both were very brave and despite their lack of stature they tormented defences in the air as well as on the ground.

Perpetual motion is the best way to describe Dougie Arnott, who came very late into the senior game. He was 25 when he signed from Pollock Juniors. Dougie has been a prolific goalscorer at all levels in the game – amateur, juvenile, junior – and now at senior level he has found his touch. He finished the 1990/91 season with 16 goals to his credit. He has certainly been one of Tommy McLean's best ever signings.

Dougie's finest contribution to the 1991 Cup campaign will probably go down on record as being his performance in the semi-final replay against Celtic. It was no surprise to anyone at that game that Paul Elliot was reported as being determined to move back south of the border. He probably wanted to get away from

Dougie celebrating a goal

Dougie Arnott, who tormented him unmercifully in the replay and also scored a fine double that evening.

Naturally Dougie is a firm favourite with the 'Well fans, who have taken him to their hearts. He quickly formed a great understanding with Iain Ferguson and they certainly benefit from their partnership. Dougie Arnott would run himself into the ground for his team-mates and his stamina is phenomenal.

Dougie is yet another player who has benefited greatly from the arrival of Davie Cooper at Fir Park. The quicksilver Arnott can read 'Coop's' intentions and anticipate the through balls from Davie. This gives him that little edge over defenders. As well as Davie Cooper, both Stevie Kirk and Phil O'Donnell have linked up to great effect with Dougie. The 3–0 victory over Rangers a mere two weeks before the Cup final was a case in point.

A local boy, Dougie hails from Carluke and he brings his own fan club to every game. His greatest fan is Davie Mathieson of Lesmahagow – Davie actually recommended Dougie to Motherwell six years before they finally signed him. 'Wasted years,' says Davie. 'We should have had Dougie Arnott at Fir Park years earlier.' Nobody took more pleasure out of that Scottish Cup victory over Celtic than Davie and he also thoroughly enjoyed that final.

Dougie Arnott epitomises everything that was good about that Cup-winning team. He has the heart of a lion and his untiring, unselfish running for his mates says it all.

IAN ANGUS

My first sight of Ian Angus was as a left-side midfield player with Eastercraigs Under-18s back in 1978. His outstanding talents were quickly spotted and he moved into senior football with Aberdeen. He picked up the award of Best Young Player in 1981 from the Second XI Association.

At Aberdeen he played over 200 games for Fergie, who rated him very highly, and he won a European Cup Winners medal with the Dons after their epic victory in Gothenberg against Real Madrid, although he was only a substitute on that memorable evening and never got on to play.

After a spell out with injury, Ian was transferred to Dundee in

Ian Angus about to score Motherwell's third goal

part exchange for Robert Connor. At Dundee he had a great deal of success but again injury interrupted his progress.

Tommy McLean signed Ian Angus at the start of season 1990/91 and he again picked up an injury which failed to clear up and which kept him on the fringe of things for most of the season. He finally shook off the injury, and with the benefit of regular games he quickly started to show exactly how good he is.

He is a very versatile player. For example, although he lined up at left back against Rangers in the 3–0 game, at Tynecastle he moved forward into midfield and scored a very good goal.

Down at Irvine where the Motherwell team went to prepare for the final, Ian Angus picked up a thigh knock. He was in fact the 'mystery man' who had picked up an injury. Fortunately Ian was passed as being fit to play on the morning of the final and in the opinion of many astute judges his was the best goal of the seven which were scored on that memorable afternoon.

Very often it can be difficult for an incoming player to win over the rather critical 'Well fans. It took Ian Angus quite some time but in the end he came good when it really mattered. Now he is one of the Cup-winning heroes and his contribution to our victory on 18 May 1991 will live on forever in the memories of all 'Well fans.

Ian Angus is without question a player of the highest quality and yet another of Tommy McLean's great signings.

IAIN FERGUSON

Natural goalscorers are an extremely scarce commodity. The ability to score goals is a gift possessed by very few. Even the coaches admit that this is one area where they fail miserably. A player can be coached in many other aspects of football, such as how to tackle, head the ball or pass with a degree of accuracy. They can be coached in running off the ball and the accepted position to take up at set pieces in order to conform to the coaching manuals. However, the gift of being in the right place at the correct time in order to put the ball past an opposing goalkeeper, while looking to be very simple, is rare indeed.

I have been privileged to watch Iain Ferguson since his formative years with Fir Park Boys' Club. Even as an 11-year-old he displayed this natural talent and ability to score goals and right throughout his career in youth football he was always a prolific goalscorer.

For reasons best known to the management at that time, Motherwell failed to capitalise on this natural asset on their own doorstep and as soon as Iain Ferguson turned 14 he was snapped up by Dundee. He duly made the grade at Dens Park and became a great favourite with the Dundee supporters. When Jock Wallace took over as manager at Ibrox, one of his first signings was Iain Ferguson, who scored the winning goal in a Skol Cup final and looked set for a great career with the Light Blues. Things didn't quite work out for Fergie though, and Jim McLean took him to Dundee United where he quickly rediscovered his goalscoring touch. Iain played in the UEFA Cup final against Gothenberg after scoring in the earlier rounds of the European tournament.

I can recall vividly a goal which was often replayed on television when 'Fergie' actually spotted the opposing goalie off his line and he had the temerity to score from over 50 yards. He was well

A young Iain Ferguson (aged 13), when he played for the successful Fir Park Boys Club. He is second from the left in the front row

Iain Ferguson celebrates his goal

inside the centre circle when he shot and the ball finished up in the net. A memorable goal indeed.

Yet again there was a hiccup in his career and eventually he was transferred to Hearts. I was right behind the goal in the European game between Hearts and Bayern Munich when Iain received a short free kick and thundered an unbeatable shot right into the roof of the Bayern net from about 30 yards. Shortly after this Alex MacDonald, who was managing Hearts at that time, relegated Iain to his reserve team. He vegetated there for over a year and even had a spell on loan with Joe Jordan's Bristol City.

Motherwell's bid of £100,000 was eventually accepted by Hearts and he joined the 'Well in November 1990. His strike rate has been highly acceptable since his arrival at Fir Park. He scored a dream of a goal against his old team-mates in the final and earned himself a deserved place in the history of Motherwell Football Club.

In an interview with the *Motherwell Times* prior to the final and headlined 'FERGIE'S HOPING FOR THIRD TIME LUCKY', Iain Ferguson revealed just what a Hampden appearance with Motherwell meant to him.

Motherwell have three players in Saturday's squad who have played in Scottish Cup finals – Davie Cooper, Iain Ferguson and Craig Paterson. And striker Ferguson is looking for third time lucky – his two previous appearances with Dundee United having ended in disappointment.

The 28-year-old was struggling to find a first-team spot at Tynecastle and viewed his transfer to Motherwell last December as a move to regular appearances.

And on reaching the Scottish Cup final in his first season at the club, he said: 'This is a real bonus and hopefully we can really give the fans something to smile about on Saturday. Obviously, I am hoping it will be third time lucky after a couple of disappointments with United. But I have also had good times at Hampden.'

Iain's Hampden highlight was scoring the only goal in the 1984 League Cup final for Rangers against Dundee United. Opponents United have failed in five Scottish Cup final visits to Hampden, but on a possible jinx, Iain said: 'I don't know if there is a jinx or not but let's hope there is. They have a lot of boys in their team who haven't been there before and they may be affected by the talk of a jinx. I never felt it myself. There was a bit of tension leading up to the games though. But we will be concentrating on how we prepare for the Cup. We have had a really good run towards the end of the season.'

A local boy from Newarthill, Iain played for Fir Park Boys' Club before joining Dundee. And on his return, he said: 'It's always difficult for a local boy coming here but I am reasonably happy about my start. But the move for me was not about money. It was to get a game and play regular first-team football, and as long as that continues I will be quite happy.'

If there is a better striker of the ball in the Premier League then I have yet to see him. Others can occasionally 'do the business' and score a cracking goal. Iain Ferguson has refined his shooting ability to an art form and I, for one, hope to be lifted out of my seat on many occasions as I cheer yet another goal from this prodigiously talented striker.

PHIL O'DONNELL

Born on 25 March 1972, Phil O'Donnell put pen to paper for Tommy McLean on 30 June 1990. He has worked his way through the youth set-up with Motherwell Boys' Club and won a string of honours in the process.

He is about 5 feet 11 inches, weighs around 10½ stone and is still growing. The feature of Phil's game which I find to be amazing is his phenomenal work-rate. I have never seen a player who could go at pace from one penalty box to the other and back again constantly for 90 minutes or, as in the case of the Cup final of 1991, for 120 minutes.

With the option of being able to bring on Colin O'Neill from the substitutes bench, everyone expected that Tommy McLean would take young Phil off and freshen up the side. The lad looked as though he was shattered after about ten minutes of extra time. Sitting in the stand watching, we made comment on the fact that Phil looked as though he had little left to offer. No sooner had the comment been made than young Phil went off again on another surging run right at the heart of the Dundee United defence. Seconds later he was back again in his own penalty area putting in a challenge and breaking up another attack. What prodigious stamina for one so young!

Mark you, this is only one aspect of his game. Phil O'Donnell

Phil O'Donnell

O'Donnell scores

has a really educated left foot, he is strong in the air, he can time his tackles to perfection, he exhibits a degree of close control and the ability to dribble past players which is rarely seen from midfield players in the modern game, and he has the knack of making telling blind-side runs which Martin Peters would have been proud of.

Discerning judges have likened Phil to Bryan Robson, and for someone who turned 19 a mere eight weeks before the Scottish Cup final, he could develop into one of the finest Scottish players for many years.

Bravery is yet another feature of his play and he showed this vividly by the courageous manner in which he scored his goal in the Cup final. Boots and bodies were flying everywhere and young Phil launched himself at the ball, headed it cleanly past the despairing Alan Main, took a knock on his head for his pains and ran a few steps before collapsing at the edge of the box. He was congratulated wildly by his mates and the trainer then applied the mandatory sponge to revive him. Seconds later he had again settled into his normal routine.

Phil has tied himself to Motherwell with a four-year contract and I only hope that this is extended right into the 21st century.

In season 1989/90 he played at Hampden in the Under-18s Amateur Cup final. Few who saw that game when Motherwell Boys' Club trounced Celtic Under-18s could have imagined just what lay in front of young Phil O'Donnell in season 1990/91. THE Andy Paton congratulated him on his return after the Scottish Cup final to Fir Park with the words, 'Well done, laddie. You probably don't realise it but you are now a legend in your own lifetime.'

DAVIE COOPER

It is acknowledged that THE 'steal of the century' was when Tommy McLean signed Davie Cooper from Rangers for £50,000 on 11 August 1989. Davie linked up again with his former team-mate Bobby Russell and to watch the magical patterns that those two can weave is a most uplifting experience.

'Coop' started his senior career with Clydebank and moved to Rangers for £100,000 where he enjoyed a degree of success which is attained in football by very few. He became a 'cult figure' and was literally worshipped by the light blue legions of supporters.

At Ibrox in 1989 he found that he was no longer in Graeme Souness's plans and the thought of performing in reserve matches in front of empty stands and terracings left him stone cold. When the opportunity arose for Davie to come to Motherwell many cynics thought that he would only play out his career with no great commitment. They couldn't have been more wrong. Davie rediscovered his appetite and zest for the game and he has turned in performances in claret and amber which have been among the highlights of my time supporting Motherwell – and I can go back about half a century!

He has a left foot which is capable of doing things with a ball which I never knew were possible. The pin-point accuracy of his crosses is awe-inspiring and a nightmare for opposing goalkeepers. When he is in possession of the ball and running at any defence he can send players the wrong way, turn them inside out and then, most importantly, he can find one of his team-mates with an inch-perfect pass or a winning lob which invariably ends up with a goal, a near miss or a great save.

Davie Cooper plays with the arrogance of a player who is well aware of his own abilities. He also has great vision and the ability to bring out the best in others. He is an entertainer in an era when regimentation and method have almost taken over. However, he is not only an entertainer, he is a lethal creator of scoring opportunities and he is no slouch at scoring himself. Who will ever forget that blistering free kick when he scored in the Skol Cup final against Aberdeen for Rangers and turned the game?

Davie is the type of player who will have fathers (who very often have stopped coming regularly to football themselves) bringing their sons to a match. Just to enable their kids to see Davie Cooper play. George Best was a similar attraction on the football field, as were Tom Finney, Stan Mathews and Jim Baxter. 'Coop' has charisma, class and quality in abundance, and since coming to Motherwell he has also shown a degree of commitment which few ever expected.

Prior to the 1991 Scottish Cup final the *Motherwell Times* discussed with Davie Cooper just what Motherwell FC and another Scottish Cup final meant to him.

Davie Cooper. He's a 'different class'

'One of the main differences between Motherwell and Rangers being in the final is that Rangers are expected to be there. Not a lot of people expect Motherwell to get to the final of the Scottish Cup and because of that the town is really buzzing. Being in the final with Motherwell means a lot to me. When I joined the club a lot of people expected me to come here and just finish my career by messing around after losing a regular place at Ibrox. If I could help Motherwell to get a Scottish Cup victory it would mean everything to me. It is a great feat for Motherwell to get there.'

Motherwell fans look at Cooper as their match winner, but on the team's other strengths, Davie said: 'I am only part of the team. It was proved in the semi-final that Motherwell don't need just Cooper. The be all and end all is that Motherwell want to win the Cup and players have grown in confidence. Dougie Arnott has had a fantastic season, the boys at the back have come on to a real steady game. And Phil O'Donnell has shown he can handle it. That's all down to confidence.' And on the prize waiting at Hampden for the winners, Davie added: 'There is so much to play for here. It would be great to win the Cup for the first time in 39 years. And wouldn't it be great for Motherwell to be in Europe and bring top European sides to Fir Park.'

What a benefit it must have been in the dressing-room to have Davie Cooper there – preparing for his 18th Cup final!

Dundee United did their utmost to negate Davie and prevent him from really turning it on in the final and, to be fair to them, they were successful to a degree. But who would have thought that Davie would have back-tracked, challenged for the ball, shut players down, headed the ball out of his own box, cleared his lines defensively and still found the time to lay on two of our four goals? He ran himself into the ground and I would doubt if any of his other Cup winning medals ever gave him more satisfaction.

Davie, mate, you are and always will be DIFFERENT CLASS!

STEVIE KIRK

Signed in 1986 from East Fife, Stevie Kirk has proved to be one of Tommy McLean's best signings. 'Kirkie' is a tall, strong midfield player who has displayed an ability to score goals at a rate which would do credit to many highly priced strikers. A few seasons ago Stevie actually finished up as second-top goalscorer in Scotland and his 18 goals were instrumental in saving Motherwell from relegation.

Just to show how versatile he is, he took over in goal with 88 minutes still to play at Tynecastle and actually saved a penalty kick to allow Motherwell to draw the match 2–2. One 'Well fan was so impressed by this that he christened his son on the Monday after this game with the totally unique middle names of 'KIRK THE GOALIE'!

Stevie picked up a nasty depressed fracture of his cheekbone in the Rangers game on 17 November 1990 in a clash with Davie Dodds. After recovering he struggled to get back into the team and then the 'Super Sub' legend started to unfold. His six-week lay-off had left Stevie short of match sharpness and on 26 January 1991 he was on the substitutes bench in the third round of the Tennents Scottish Cup against Aberdeen at Pittodrie.

Motherwell played particularly well that day with John Philliben being a real stalwart in defence. The match produced football of the highest calibre. Aberdeen played their usual accurate passing, probing game and Motherwell were under sustained pressure from the Dons. Fast breakaways by the raiding 'Well forwards kept the game very finely balanced and it soon became quite apparent that whichever team scored the opening goal would be favourites to move into the fourth round of the tournament.

The referee awarded Motherwell a free kick for a foul about 30 yards out from goal and before it could be taken Tommy McLean made the substitution of the season. Iain Ferguson limped off and Stevie Kirk trotted on. As he left the dug-out the manager instructed him to 'use your height at the back post'.

'I'm going to score here,' Stevie stated with conviction and moved on to the park. He ran up until he was square with Davie Cooper, who feinted as though he was going to send in a cross but instead simply rolled the ball in front of Stevie Kirk. 'Kirkie' glanced up and without hesitation sent an unstoppable left-foot shot screaming high into the Aberdeen net. Theo Snelders miraculously managed to get the faintest of touches on the ball but he was comprehensively beaten by the sheer pace of the shot.

For many, this will go down as being the goal of the season but there were many other gems to come from Motherwell in the 1991 Tennents Scottish Cup Competition.

Stevie Kirk simply couldn't contain his elation and he set off on a mini lap of honour behind the goals at the Beach End of the park. The referee took a dim view of this act of 'leaving the field of play without permission' and promptly brought the celebrations to a halt by showing Stevie a yellow card.

Thirty seconds on the park and he had scored with his first touch and been booked for his over-enthusiastic celebrations. The Super-Sub legend had been born!

In the fourth round of the Cup against Falkirk Stevie Kirk again came off the subs bench and scored – this time with his second touch of the ball.

The next tie, against Morton, proved to be a really dour encounter at Fir Park. Stevie Kirk played in the number 12 jersey but when he was brought on he found himself instantly picked up by two Morton players and the game ended in a goalless draw.

At Cappielow in the replay Stevie played for the whole 120 minutes. With the score at 1–1 a penalty shoot-out decided the tie. Kirk kept up his record of scoring in every round of the Cup by notching one from the penalty spot. Motherwell squeezed through by five penalties to four in their most difficult tie of the tournament. It was an old 'Well favourite, Johnny Gahagan, who had scored against his former team-mates to keep Morton's hopes alive and Johnny also scored with his penalty.

On the day of the final, Tommy McLean received a letter from Johnny Gahagan in which he wished Motherwell all the best in the final against Dundee United. He said that he would have given anything to be out there playing in claret and amber and, typically, he also commiserated with those members of the pool who failed to be chosen in the final 13. This gesture was really appreciated.

A total of 41,765 saw Motherwell fight out a dour goalless draw against Celtic at Hampden Park on 3 April, but the crowd of 31,317 for the replay on 10 April was treated to a really superlative football match.

Celtic opened up as though they were going to run right over the top of Motherwell. They had the ball in the net within a few minutes only to see the linesman's flag raised to deny them the opening goal. Not for long, however. A crazy mix-up over a corner from the left wing saw Tommy Boyd scoring through his own posts.

Dougie Arnott scored an opportunist goal to bring the game to 1–1 and then Anton Rogan reasserted Celtic's lead with a crashing shot into the Motherwell net: 2–1 at half time and everything to play for.

Stevie Kirk scores the winning goal in the 1991 Tennents Scottish Cup final (Picture: courtesy of Douglas McKendrick, Wishaw Press)

Stevie Kirk celebrates the winner

Tommy McLean took off Ian Angus who had sustained a knock and pushed on Stevie Kirk shortly after the interval. Eleven minutes into the second half Dougie Arnott scored with a brilliant header from a Luc Nijholt cross to level the match. The initiative was slipping away from Celtic but Tom Boyd hirpled off and Nick Cusack came on to the park. Tommy McLean reorganised his team as Celtic continued to throw everything into attack.

Stevie Kirk received the ball out on the left and touched it inside to Colin O'Neill, and the Irishman, who was 35 yards out, thundered the ball into the Celtic net: 3–2 and Celtic were in deep trouble.

However, more was to come when Super-Sub Stevie Kirk took a pass from young Phil O'Donnell. From the corner of the penalty box Stevie looked up and coolly lobbed the ball over Paddy Bonner, who was a yard or so off his line. The ball rattled off the back stanchion and rebounded into play. Referee Douglas Hope immediately awarded the goal.

A mere five minutes left to play and Motherwell were home and dry. Well, that is probably the wrong way to describe this victory which was played in torrential rain for the whole 90 minutes. Dougie Arnott, who scored twice, was voted Man of the Match.

The final was five minutes into extra time with the score standing at 3–3 when Super-Sub Kirk again scored after coming off the bench, heading home a Davie Cooper corner kick to take the score to 4–3.

Stevie Kirk had found the net in every round of the Cup. It was only fitting that having scored with that first touch against Aberdeen Stevie should get the ultimate winner in the final.

Football folklore is full of incidents and events. One thing certain is that it took Motherwell 39 years before they could get their hands on the Scottish Cup trophy again. I confidently forecast that they will not have as long to wait until their third victory in a Scottish Cup final. Stevie Kirk's contribution to this second Cup victory can never be understated and 'Well fans will forever be in his debt. Long after Stevie Kirk has hung up his boots, fans will fondly recall his great goals in every round including the final in 1991 when Motherwell won the Cup by four goals to three against Dundee United.

COLIN O'NEILL

It was as an outside right that Colin O'Neill was introduced to Irish football with Ards in 1980 as a 16-year-old. 'I was a flying winger,' laughed Colin. 'You had to be quick to avoid some of those tackles from determined, experienced full backs.'

Altogether, Colin played for Ards, Larne, Ballymena United and Portadown. 'I had more clubs than Tommy Docherty,' joked Colin. 'I was delighted when I got the chance to come to Scotland and play for Motherwell,' he said. At that time he was carrying a bit of excess weight, but Tommy McLean soon worked this off him and he blossomed into a far better player than he had ever been before. His form brought him International honours for Northern Ireland and I would predict that he will win many more caps for his country.

'Tell me about that semi-final goal, Colin,' I asked.

'I just looked up and hit it,' he stated. 'I heard someone shout for me to put the ball out to Nicky Cusack who had moved out to the wing but I just decided to have a go! When the ball landed in the net I realised that I had beaten Paddy Bonner with the best goal I have ever scored in my life! And from at least 35 yards out.

'Luc Nijholt prevented me from performing my usual head-spring with a tackle that I would have been proud of. Celtic never recovered from this killer blow and when "Kirkie" scored the fourth goal we all knew that we were going all the way!'

In the final Colin O'Neill had a new experience. It was the first time in the season that he had been chosen as a substitute. He said that it was the most nerve-wracking experience of his life. In actual fact he never sat down throughout the whole game and part of the time was passed by conducting the choir behind the goal at the Motherwell end. This really lifted the team, particularly when the score reached 3–3.

Colin's was one of the longest warm-ups in football – it lasted 117 minutes. 'I only played for three minutes and I think I only got three kicks at the ball; still, it was the hardest game of my life. After the final whistle we started to celebrate and at the time of this interview [three weeks later] the celebrations are still continuing,' said Colin with an infectious smile.

The style of play in Scotland suits Colin's committed attitude and he enjoys a tremendous rapport with the fans, who seem to identify with him. They took to him right away when he first came to Fir Park.

Another pressure goal which Colin scored was his penalty kick against Morton. The score after extra time was 4−4 on penalties and if Colin scored, the 'Well would be through to play Celtic at Hampden in the semi-final.

Tommy McLean signalled to Colin to calm down just before he left the centre circle. On the long walk up to the penalty spot Colin joined in with the 'Well fans as they chanted, 'PSYCHO, PSYCHO, PSYCHO, PSYCHO!' On reaching the box he took a deep breath, blew out his cheeks, then ran up and hammered the ball into the net. He next performed a double somersault before being mobbed by the ecstatic Motherwell fans.

They were on their way to Hampden.

Colin O'Neill is one of those totally committed players. He has an irrepressible sense of humour and he lifts his mates before, during and after every game.

Colin would like to go on record and thank Mr McSween, the surgeon who so skilfully operated on his knee a mere 14 days before the final. Without his expertise there is no way that Colin could have been involved in that Hampden climax.

THE INCONSOLABLES

Tommy McLean had a squad of 18 down at Irvine. The five who failed to get the nod must have been inconsolable at missing out on the opportunity to play in the greatest game of their lives.

John Philliben had been 'Man of the Match' at Aberdeen and he performed real heroics at the heart of the 'Well defence against Celtic in the semi-finals.

Nicky Cusack had scored a great double against Falkirk and he also helped turn the game when he came on for the injured Tom Boyd in the semi-final replay.

Joe McLeod also scored an excellent goal against Falkirk and *Jamie Dolan* had a great game in the third round match against Aberdeen. Only *Stevie Bryce* of the 18-strong squad hadn't featured in the run-in to the final. All the others must have felt really 'gutted' when Tommy McLean told them that they were not in the 13 for the big game.

Bobby Russell, who had been a substitute against both Aber-

Colin O'Neill celebrates his wonder goal from 35 yards against Celtic in the semi-final replay (Picture: Courtesy of Craig Halkett, Daily Record)

deen and Falkirk, also played his part in winning the Cup. He played against Morton and he was one of the five successful scorers from the penalty spot. Now in the twilight of his career Bobby quite simply couldn't reach peak fitness in time to be considered for the final.

In my opinion Bobby is one of the finest players ever to wear the claret and amber. He oozes sheer class and when playing with his mate, Davie Cooper, they are the perfect blend.

Every time I watch Bobby Russell play I feel as though I have just won a bonus. His appearances were quite rare in season 1990/91 but who can ever forget that Russell shimmy in the opening game of that League campaign when he ran into the Celtic penalty area with the ball at his feet. He dipped his shoulder. Anton Rogan 'bought it' and proceeded to knock Pat

Bonner on to his back as he fell over the goalkeeper. Bobby laughed as he gleefully passed the ball into the empty Celtic net from six yards. A typical Russell goal.

Yes, each and every one of these 'extra' players played a vital part in the winning of the Scottish Cup by Motherwell in 1991 and although they hurt deeply for themselves they KNOW that without their efforts Motherwell could have had another year without a trophy. So does every 'Well fan.

Nicky Cusack

Bobby Russell celebrating with Tam Boyd after scoring the only goal of the game against Rangers at Fir Park

Chapter Ten

THE OPPOSITION

It is fitting here to say a few words about the Dundee United players who contributed so much to make the 1991 Scottish Cup final the epic match that it was.

Alan Main, at 23, is quite young to be an established Premier League goalkeeper but he has earned the number one jersey on merit. He is a very safe last line of defence with great reflexes and tremendous concentration. He has already built up a tremendous reputation and his kick-outs are enormous. Many goals have been scored by United due to his enormous clearances up the park. Jim McLean signed him for £7,000 from Elgin City.

John Clark is now 26. He originally started his career as a forward but he has now been converted to defence. He possesses the ability to hit a dead ball with devastating force. A really strong, hard player who always gives 100 per cent, he scored in the semi-final at Dunfermline against St Johnstone.

Maurice Malpas, the Scotland defender, is probably at his peak at 28 years of age. He has been voted by the sports writers as their Player of the Year. He is now the team captain and his play is marked by his coolness and composure under pressure. He reads the game very well and is a fine example for any youngster taking up the game.

Jim McInally is a superb midfield player. Now 27, he started his career at Parkhead with Celtic before moving on to Dundee and then Nottingham Forest. He joined United for a fee of £130,000 which included Dave Bowman. He is a very keen competitor who enjoys his role in the United midfield.

Bowman and Clark in action in the final

Miodrag Krivokapic, a 31-year-old defender, was signed for £200,000 from Niksic Crnagora. Gordon Wallace once said that he was the finest professional player that he had ever worked with and that is high praise indeed. It took him a long time to settle in Scotland but he has shown what a superb player he is.

Dave Bowman, at 28, is a fiery player who always excels whenever the going gets tough. His father starred for Hearts and Dave has inherited all of Andy Bowman's skill and tenacity. He came to United along with McInally but hasn't enjoyed the same degree of success, although many good judges think that he is the better player of the two.

Freddy Van der Hoorn, 27, signed from Den Bosch and cost United £200,000. A regular scorer and deadly with free kicks, he is a great favourite with the fans. Typically, like many other Dutch players, he is very comfortable on the ball.

Ray McKinnon is still only 20 but this lad is my favourite

Dundee United player. However, going by the number of occasions that he is either given a sub's jersey or substituted during a game, Jim McLean doesn't agree with my opinion. Or perhaps this is all part of Jim's learning process for young Ray? A joy to behold whenever he is in possession, he has the ability to score with either foot. He is a really tremendous prospect.

Hamish French is a versatile player and another product of the Highland League. Picked up from Keith for a mere £10,000, he has played up front and in midfield. He could do with a bit of good luck because he has been dogged by injuries since he arrived at Tannadice.

Duncan Ferguson, the 19-year-old striker, first caught my eye last season when he helped the United Under-18 team knock Motherwell out of the BP Cup. At 6 feet 2 inches he has a big advantage in the air and he uses his height to great effect. He fills the role once occupied by Davie Dodds. Like all good strikers he is always among the goals and he will score many goals in the years ahead, providing he avoids injury of course.

Darren Jackson, 24 years old, also cost Jim McLean £200,000. He moved from Meadowbank to Newcastle United before joining up at Tannadice. One of the most lethal strikers in the Premier League, he is very quick and hard to pin down. He never knows when he is beaten.

John O'Neil, 19, is a tricky winger who has a tremendous future ahead of him, one that Motherwell missed because he did star with the Fir Park Boys' Club. He is very deceptive on the ball and also knows where the goals lie!

Billy McKinley is a 22-year-old who already has a wealth of first-team experience. He has also caught Andy Roxburgh's eye. A beautiful passer of a ball, he also has great perception and vision. When he matures he will be outstanding.

Dundee United were late-comers into the Scottish scene, in 1923, although they had in fact been in existence since 1906 under the name of Dundee Hibernian. Obviously the change of name was an attempt to alter the overall image of the club, which had its origins in the Irish immigrant community, and to appeal to a less sectarian group in a time when bigotry was far more pronounced than at present. To be fair, they seem to have managed to achieve

Andy Paton

their aim because outwith Dundee itself there is little knowledge as to the 'roots' of the club.

They gained promotion from the Second Division in 1925 but they never really managed to consolidate in the top flight until Jerry Kerr – a former Motherwell centre-half – came on to the scene at Tannadice.

Jerry Kerr had been signed by 'Sailor' Hunter from the long-defunct St Bernards just before the outbreak of the 1939–45 war. On his return from the forces, Jerry had to be content to be reserve to Andrew Paton and his appearances in the top team were usually limited to whenever Andy Paton was under suspension. Like most good players Andy missed very few games due to being injured.

Jerry Kerr was Dundee United's manager from 1959 right through to 1971 and during this time he consolidated and he brought a good number of Scandinavian players to Dundee. This added extra spice to the top flight in Scottish football.

After Jim McLean took over Dundee United in 1971 they really emerged as a force to be reckoned with. Never relegated from the Premier League, they have built and re-built top quality teams during Jim's 20-year tenure in office. He has of course been a director at Tannadice for a number of years and, indeed, he is now chairman/manager of this great club.

On 5 September 1925, Motherwell and Dundee United met for the very first time and the result was a 1–1 draw in the League at Tannadice. In the return game at Fir Park, the 'Well won 4–0 in convincing fashion. Early matches tended to favour Motherwell but in recent years the pendulum has swung in favour of the 'Tangerines'. At the time of writing, Motherwell have gone 21 games at Tannadice without a single victory.

As you will see from the list of results, there were long gaps during which both teams didn't play one another because they were in different divisions.

Motherwell recorded their biggest ever win over the Tannadice side when they beat Dundee United by 12–1 at Fir Park in season 1953/54. Wilson Humphries scored six goals that day while Jackie Hunter had to be content with four goals. The other two goals came from the penalty spot, both converted by Willie Redpath.

I will always remember the glee on the face of one of my mates, Hugh Lumsden, when Motherwell made the score 11–1. In our factory, as was common practice in those days, we had an 11–goal accumulator and more or less everyone contributed their shilling every week into this sweepstake. Every member received a team and they totalled up the goals which their team scored each week until someone reached 11 goals. They would win 'the accumulator'.

Hugh Lumsden had drawn Motherwell during that week and it looked at that point as though he had won the works accumulator in its very first week. Suddenly the referee pointed to the penalty spot and Hugh, seeing his little pot of gold slipping away, immediately questioned the referee's parentage.

The score finished at 12–1 and poor Hughie Lumsden had to settle for the fact that Motherwell had really gone over the top as far as the 11-goal accumulator was concerned. He had to settle for only ONE goal to his credit.

It was reported that the Dundee United goalkeeper, Edminston, who had just returned from a tour of duty in Korea for his National Service, actually contemplated volunteering for another spell of duty out there. He is alleged to have said that there was less fire-power in Korea than there was at Fir Park on that day.

	P	W	D	L	F	A
MOTHERWELL (FIR PARK)	43	17	6	20	77	63
DUNDEE UTD (TANNADICE)	44	23	15	6	85	40

(MOTHERWELL GOALS LISTED FIRST)

	HOME	AWAY		HOME	AWAY
1925/26	4–0	1–1	1977/78	0–0	2–3
1926/27	6–0	1–0		0–1	1–1
1929/30	6–1	1–1	1978/79	0–1	1–2
1931/32	5–0	6–1		0–4	1–2
1953/54	12–1	0–1	1982/83	0–2	0–5
1960/61	4–3	1–0		1–4	0–4
1961/62	2–1	1–1	1983/84	2–2	0–4
1962/63	0–0	1–2		1–3	1–2
1963/64	0–3	1–4	1985/86	0–1	0–3
1964/65	1–1	1–3		2–0	0–4
1965/66	0–3	1–5	1986/87	0–2	0–4
1966/67	1–1	1–1		1–0	0–2
1967/68	1–3	1–1	1987/88	2–1	1–1
1969/70	0–2	0–0		4–2	1–3
1970/71	1–2	2–2	1988/89	1–2	1–1
1971/72	0–1	0–2		1–2	1–1
1972/73	1–4	2–1	1989/90	3–2	1–1
1973/74	4–0	1–0		0–1	1–1
1974/75	0–1	0–5	1990/91	0–2	0–1
1975/76	2–1	1–1		1–0	0–3
	3–2	4–1			
1976/77	4–0	0–2			
	1–1	1–1			

Over and above the League matches there have been a few cup clashes, the most memorable being the 1965 Summer Cup encounter when Motherwell won 3–1 at Fir Park and Dundee United won 1–0 at Tannadice. Motherwell won the cup with a 3–2 aggregate score. There was a capacity attendance at Dundee and the majority of the crowd were supporting Motherwell. The road home was choc-a-bloc with 'Well fans with claret and amber scarves waving out of their car windows.

If there is a good game being played and Motherwell are not in action themselves, it is normal practice for my circle of friends to go along and enjoy the match. We normally take in such games as the Junior Cup semi-finals and final, any European cup-ties plus a wide range of First and Second Division midweek games and all Internationals.

For quite some time, Dundee United captured the imagination and regular midweek runs to Tannadice to see teams such as Barcelona and Gothenburg became the norm.

The 'Arabs' enjoyed a magnificent run in Europe when they reached the final and on the day before their away leg in the final against Gothenburg my radio at work was tuned in to Radio Clyde. Paul Cooney announced that there were still a few seats left on one of the flights going to Sweden and gave a contact number for Harry Hynds Travel. A quick phone call and that was everything organised. The flight was leaving from Glasgow at 11 a.m. on the day of the final and returning at 11 p.m. on the same day.

When Tommy McLean heard that I was going to see his brother's team he phoned Jim and arranged for me to meet him at the team's hotel in Gothenburg at 2 p.m. Jim would have a good ticket for me. The travel package did include a seat at the match but this sounded like a better offer and I delightedly accepted.

The small high-wing monoplane was filled with fans and it was a pleasant flight over to Sweden. Gothenburg is a very beautiful city, if rather expensive. I made my way to the Dundee United team's hotel and Jim McLean appeared in the foyer promptly at 2 p.m. I wished him good luck as he handed over the envelope containing my ticket and then moved on to chat with some of the Press corps who were enjoying the affluence of their expense account surroundings.

After a nice meal which set me back about £30 – about 300 per cent more expensive than Glasgow – I made my way to the magnificent Ullevi Stadium. Obtaining a cushion upon entry, I soon located my seat and enjoyed the 'music' from a loud pop group playing from the back of a lorry parked behind the goals. The friendly Swedes worked hard at enjoying their final and I have never before or since seen so many faces painted as there were in the blue and white colours of Gothenburg. The overall standards of the ground made me feel embarrassed when I thought of Hampden Park and its environs!

'What are you doing here, John?' a voice enquired and, turning round, I saw Archie McPherson who was covering the match for television. He was down from his TV platform savouring the atmosphere of the ground prior to the kick-off.

'Just over to see a good game, Archie,' I replied and after exchanging a few pleasantries Archie moved on.

One thing really struck me about the Swedes – at least 90 per cent of them seem to have mastery of the English language.

As to the game itself, Dundee United lost a goal and then seemed to settle for a narrow defeat with the object of winning the home leg. On that evening, if they had attacked Gothenburg I am certain that they would have scored a goal or two because their defence didn't seem to be their strongest area as a team. The lone figure of Iain Ferguson ploughing a solitary path up front is my abiding memory of this match. A more cavalier approach would certainly have resulted in Dundee United actually winning a European trophy instead of just coming close once again.

After the game I made my way to the pick-up point, boarded the plane and I was back home in East Kilbride at 1 a.m. after a memorable day's outing.

We all know that Dundee United failed to pull back that single goal advantage in the second leg of the final, and I was one of the thousands who applauded the Swedes from the park to earn Dundee United a monetary award from UEFA for good behaviour.

The same over-cautious tactics saw Dundee United lose the Scottish Cup final to Celtic a week or so later at Hampden. They tried and failed to hold on to a one-goal lead and Celtic scored two very late goals to again disappoint Jim McLean's team.

They learned their lesson and they certainly weren't defensive in the 4–3 final against Motherwell.

Chapter Eleven

MINUTE BY MINUTE

In my book on the history of the 'Steelmen', I concluded by writing a section entitled 'Minute by Minute' and this referred to the minutes of board meetings at Motherwell Football Club. I had managed to obtain the club's records of all board meetings from 1910 to 1975 and read through all these books to pick out excerpts which I felt would be of interest to readers. In this chapter I include a similarly headed section but this time I am highlighting features of the Cup final and the times at which they took place.

Jock Brown, the BBC match commentator, was impressed by the fantastic family atmosphere for the final, pointing out that the crowd had arrived very early to savour the occasion. The cameras panned around the ground picking out fancy dress outfits such as giant teddy bears in claret and amber, Dundee United fans dressed as Arabs, banners declaring 'Motherwell Supporters – LUTON Branch', 'Fintry Arabs', 'Argyll Bar Arabs', 'Young Ardler Arabs', etc.

I have never before seen such a vast number of claret and amber jerseys and favours and scarves together at the one time. The same can be said of the tangerine and black. Balloons at either end of the park were released – tangerine and black balloons at the Dundee United end and claret and amber ones at the Motherwell end.

Preceded by the ball boys, brothers Jim and Tommy McLean led out their teams together. They lined up in their designated positions in front of the fair play posters.

Peter Gardiner, the SFA President, led out John Chapman, the Motherwell chairman, and Harry Leadbetter, representing Dundee United, followed by Jim Farry, the chief executive of the SFA and John Hamilton from Tennents. They were quickly introduced to all the players and match officials.

The players, as soon as the formalities were over, quickly went to their respective ends of the park – Dundee United to the east end and Motherwell to the west end, to salute their fans prior to the kick-off.

David Syme brought the team captains to the centre of the park. Maurice Malpas won the toss and elected to kick from right to left when viewing from the grandstand. The teams were:

DUNDEE UNITED	MOTHERWELL
1 ALAN MAIN	1 ALASTAIR MAXWELL
2 JOHN CLARK	2 LUC NIJHOLT
3 MAURICE MALPAS	3 TOM BOYD
4 JIM McINALLY	4 JIM GRIFFIN
5 MIODRAG KRIVOKAPIC	5 CRAIG PATERSON
6 DAVE BOWMAN	6 CHRIS McCART
7 FREDDY VAN DER HOORN	7 DOUGIE ARNOTT
8 RAY McKINNON	8 IAN ANGUS
9 HAMISH FRENCH	9 IAIN FERGUSON
10 DUNCAN FERGUSON	10 PHIL O'DONNELL
11 DARREN JACKSON	11 DAVIE COOPER
12 JOHN O'NEIL	12 STEVIE KIRK
14 BILLY McKINLEY	14 COLIN O'NEILL

The first five minutes of the game are analysed here minute by minute and it is surprising to find the amount of action which can be packed into 60 seconds of play. To cover the whole match in this manner would entail a great deal of time being devoted to the normal probing and mundane incidents which are part and parcel of every game but which do not merit the rating of highlights. From 3.05 on, a more general coverage of the game will be given. Only where incidents of prominence occur will a more detailed report be resorted to.

3.00

Dougie Arnott got the game underway by touching the ball to Iain Ferguson, who pushed the ball square to Davie Cooper on Motherwell's left wing. Davie was instantly tackled by Dave Bowman who won the ball and touched it inside to Darren Jackson. He turned the ball back to John Clark. Clark lofted the ball forward and it went out of play about ten yards from the corner flag. Tom Boyd quickly shied the ball to Davie Cooper who nodded it back to him. The ball bounced awkwardly and Tam 'sclaffed' the ball high in the air towards his own penalty area. Craig Paterson headed the ball out of the danger zone and 'Coop' touched the ball back to his captain. Boyd lobbed the ball up the line to Dougie Arnott who was immediately challenged from the back by Krivokapic. David Syme instantly blew for the first foul of the game. Tom Boyd lifted the ball forward towards the corner flag but Van der Hoorn, who was policing Arnott, allowed the ball to drift out harmlessly for a bye-kick.

3.01

Alan Main launched the ball up the field and Phil O'Donnell rose and headed the ball to his left while under pressure from McKinnon. The ball was headed back by big Duncan Ferguson to Jim McInally, who released a superb pass right into the path of Hamish French. The accuracy and 'weight' of the pass was such that it left the 'Well defenders stranded as Hamish surged through towards the unprotected Maxwell. He took a quick touch to steady himself as the ball reached the edge of the box and, from 12 yards, he slotted the ball home inside Maxie's right hand post and turned away with his hands held aloft in jubilation. The game had only been in motion for 80 seconds and he had found the net.

David Syme blew his whistle and gave offside against Darren Jackson who, to be fair, was at least a clear yard offside at the moment McInally played the ball forward. Chris McCart took the free kick which went straight to Krivokapic who headed the ball clear. It bounced out for a shy just inside the United half of the park and Luc Nijholt hurried to throw the ball back into play.

Tommy McLean and his brother Jim lead their teams out

3.02

Jim Griffin received the ball and touched it back to the Dutchman who instantly returned it to him. Jim controlled it with one touch and pushed the ball out to the wing for Iain Ferguson. He was challenged by Malpas and Duncan Ferguson. The latter hit the ball out of play off the shin of Malpas. This time Luc gave a longer throw inside to Arnott who touched the ball inside to Ian Angus. Dave Bowman intercepted the pass and the ball again went out of play for a shy. The throw from Luc was back-headed on by 'Griff', who found Fergie. He touched it with his head back to Jim Griffin who hurriedly lofted it forward. It was deflected to Iain Ferguson and he touched it before it went out of play. He laughed as the linesman awarded Motherwell the throw-in. Luc found Davie Cooper who had wandered over to the Motherwell right wing and Davie sent in a curling cross which went out of play at the far side of the United penalty area.

3.03

Alan Main again punted the bye-kick into the centre circle where it was met by the tall Chris McCart, who outjumped Duncan Ferguson.

The ball broke to O'Donnell and it bounced before McInally toe-poked it high in the air for big Chris to head clear again. The ball was met by Malpas who glanced it inside the centre circle for Ian Angus to touch it on to Ray McKinnon. He turned it out for a shy on the far side of the park. Tom Boyd threw the ball back to Paterson who squared it to Alastair Maxwell.

3.04

Maxie tapped the ball to Luc. He slotted the ball through to McCart who found Griffin. 'Griff' attempted to play the ball back to Chris but it went out of play off Duncan Ferguson. Big Chris threw the ball to Iain Ferguson and from there it moved from Griffin to O'Donnell, to Angus, to Boyd, who moved it on to 'Coop' who was instantly dispossessed by John Clark. Nijholt read Clark's pass well, intercepted and played the ball to McCart, who hammered it high towards the United penalty area. Dougie Arnott was adjudged to have backed into Van der Hoorn and the free kick went to United.

3.05

Phil O'Donnell's long leg got to the resultant free kick before Ray McKinnon and, under pressure from Arnott, Krivokapic touched the ball back to his keeper. Main threw the ball out to Van der Hoorn who surged forward into the 'Well half of the park and squared the ball out to his right to John Clark. He moved it on up the wing to Bowman and the two interchanged passes again before Bowman found French out at the right corner flag. Luc Nijholt tackled hard and forced the ball out for a shy. Dave Bowman, the long throw expert, lined up to heave the ball into the 'Well box.

3.06

Dougie Arnott upended Freddie Van der Hoorn who was surging forward into the 'Well half of the park.

3.09

Luc Nijholt was judged to have fouled Hamish French when he tackled him from the back. John Clark lined up to take the free kick but it was Jim McInally who took the kick and squared the ball to Van der Hoorn. From almost 30 yards out the Dutchman, who has earned a reputation for his ability to shoot accurately from long range, thundered in a hard shot low to Maxie's right. The ball beat the diving goalkeeper but struck the bottom of the upright and spun right across the goalmouth between Alastair Maxwell and his goal line before going out of play beyond the far post for a bye kick.

Freddie Van der Hoorn shook his head in utter disbelief at this cruel piece of bad luck which deprived his team from taking an early lead. This only served to convince almost everyone inside Hampden that once again in a Cup final it simply wasn't going to be Dundee United's day – the jinx had struck yet again.

3.12

Motherwell rallied at this point and the tireless Dougie Arnott forced a corner. Alan Main, under pressure from Arnott, fumbled Davie Cooper's wicked in-swinger and the ball broke to Chris McCart, who fired it just wide of the United goal. However, David Syme spotted an infringement and blew for a foul on Alan Main. Dougie Arnott was proving to be a real thorn in United's flesh as he continually harassed their defence.

3.13

Davie Cooper coolly flicked a ball to Tommy Boyd just inside the centre circle and Tommy set up a half chance for Phil O'Donnell. At the other end it took a superbly timed tackle by Nijholt to thwart Hamish French as he closed in on goal after a fine low through ball from John Clark. The game continued to swing from end to end as both teams struggled to gain ascendancy.

3.19

Arnott swung in a delightful cross and big Craig Paterson who was up in support just failed to connect properly. The ball went over Main's crossbar for a bye kick.

Seconds later Darren Jackson did the same at the other end. Neither side was giving an inch but slowly and surely Motherwell were coming more and more into the game.

3.24

United won a throw-in near to the corner flag on the right wing and this signalled yet another of Bowman's prodigiously long throws. John Clark made poor contact with the ball which ricocheted through a sea of legs to Ray McKinnon. As he attempted to get his shot in on goal from about eight yards out, Maxwell threw himself bravely at McKinnon's feet to smother the ball and effect a very sound save.

Jim Griffin and Jim McInally were fiercely competing for every ball. It was developing into a classic encounter between two well-matched, strong-tackling midfielders. No quarter was being asked or given and the spirit of their clashes was one of the highlights of an extremely hard-fought match. There was never any sign of petty play-acting from either of these two basically honest players and their confrontations were a joy for the purists to watch.

3.29

Two corners inside a minute – one from the left and another from the right – underlined the fact that the tide could be turning in 'Well's favour.

3.30

On the half hour mark a mazy run from Davie Cooper worried the Dundee United defence.

3.33

Luc Nijholt lifted a high ball deep into the opposition's half of the park and Krivokapic, under pressure from Arnott, headed the ball

Fergie scores the opening goal

out but only as far as Ian Angus, who headed the ball back to young O'Donnell. Phil chested the ball down and touched it on to Iain Ferguson. Fergie quickly switched the ball out to Jim Griffin on the right wing and immediately turned and made a great run into the Dundee United penalty box. 'Griff' swung in a superb cross which took the slightest of deflections on its way to the far post. Iain Ferguson timed his run and jump to perfection and met the cross squarely with his head to bullet the ball high into the top right-hand corner of Alan Main's goal.

The deadlock was broken and the jubilant Motherwell players engulfed Fergie as they congratulated him for scoring a memorable opening goal. There was a thunderous roar from the 'Well fans. Totally delirious, they chanted, shouted, sang and cheered right through to the interval.

3.40

Tackling became even fiercer and Davie Cooper was grounded by John Clark. Ian Angus crunched in on Ray McKinnon and Maxie lined up his wall for the free kick. Dougie Arnott blocked the shot and the danger was cleared.

3.43

Krivokapic fouled Dougie Arnott as the tempo of the match actually increased and became even more frenzied. Phil O'Donnell continually made telling supporting runs which maintained the pressure on the Dundee United defence.

Just before half-time Maxie made a rare error when he failed fully to get to a cross from the United right. He managed to get the slightest of touches to the ball and it was scrambled clear.

3.45

David Syme brought a hectic first half to a close.

Motherwell, after an edgy start in which they survived an offside goal and a freak deflection off the base of the upright from Van der Hoorn, had gained in both confidence and composure as the game progressed. After the lift which they received when Iain Ferguson scored the opening goal, the advantage definitely lay with Motherwell at the interval.

I have no doubt in my mind that the game was won and lost when Fergie found the net in the 33rd minute. Had Dundee United scored first I am certain that they would have 'shut the game down' in their own inimitable manner. They would have 'killed the game off' as they retained possession, passing back to their 'keeper and generally time-wasting the game to a total stand-still. This has been a feature of their play in recent years and they are past masters at this aspect of the game. It frustrates the opposition and when they become over-extended in their anxiety to equalise, Dundee United generally hit with a sucker punch. Not attractive to watch, but exceptionally effective, these tactics have stood them in good stead over the years. Yes indeed, it was imperative that Motherwell score first if they were to prevent the Dundee United 'machine' from taking over.

While the opening 45 minutes had been hard-fought and thrill-a-minute stuff with end-to-end play, nothing had happened to prepare us for the second half which we were about to experience. This second phase of the match epitomised everything that is good in our Scottish game and I for one can't recall a more totally enthralling 45 minutes, especially when you remember the high stakes for which both teams were playing.

3.55

Jim McLean left big Duncan Ferguson in the dressing-room after the interval and brought on John O'Neil who had played for the Fir Park Boys' Club before signing on at Tannadice.

Motherwell played calmly at the start of the second half but Paul Sturrock's boys were, if anything, putting in even more effort than before. Dave Bowman caught the eye. He was prominent in most of the early moves, always challenging, prompting and probing for an opening.

Tom Boyd was given plenty of opportunity to show his fine turn of speed, which he used to good effect to break up a series of United moves.

4.00

John O'Neil lofted a high ball into the penalty area. Alastair Maxwell came sharply off his line and stretched high in the air to reach the cross. John Clark had also seen the O'Neil cross coming over and he came thundering in towards the 'Well goal and collided with Maxwell as he jumped high for the ball. At the point of impact, Clark appeared to turn side on and his hip bone made contact with Ally's stomach. The ball broke out of the box and went out of play for a shy.

David Syme signalled for Bobby Holmes to come on to the park to attend to the prostrate Maxwell and the game was held up for quite some time as the referee gave Ally every chance to recover. As the game resumed, Maxie was obviously struggling and United put him under pressure at every opportunity. John O'Neil was posing fresh problems for the 'Well defence with his great close control and ability to send in telling crosses.

Davie Cooper won the ball in the inside-left position on the

Luc Nijholt

halfway line and broke clear with Dougie Arnott in attendance. Dougie darted away from his marker to give Davie a target. Davie dwelt on the ball for a split second too long. When he released his pass to Dougie it took the slightest of deflections and a promising move broke down.

4.05

From Main's clearance up the park the ball broke to Dave Bowman wide on the right. He touched the ball forward, steadied himself and sent in a hard low shot to the far side of the goal. Maxie seemed to be a bit slow in getting down as the shot beat him and finished up nestling in the back of the net.

Now the scoreline stood at 1–1 and the Arabs on the east terracing celebrated the equaliser. We were all certain that a fully fit Maxwell would have saved this shot with ease. Nevertheless, the initiative seemed to have swung in favour of United who really had their tails up now.

A combined challenge on Jim Griffin by John O'Neil and Ray McKinnon resulted in a foul being awarded.

4.09

Davie Cooper took the free kick from about 35 yards out and sent in one of those swinging, tantalising, swerving crosses which are a hallmark of his play. Under pressure from Craig Paterson, John Clark misheaded the ball back across his own six-yard box. Phil O'Donnell launched himself through a ruck of players and flailing boots to head the ball cleanly into the net, high past the helpless Alan Main. An exceptionally fine and brave goal from an exceptionally talented young player. He took a knock in the process of scoring and collapsed at the edge of the penalty area. 2–1 and the 'Well fans came alive again.

4.13

Tommy McLean made a substitution. He took off the opening goalscorer, Iain Ferguson, and brought on 'Super-Sub' Stevie Kirk.

4.15

Within minutes a ball from Davie Cooper found Stevie Kirk on the edge of Dundee United's box and he cleverly touched it back to the on-rushing Ian Angus, who took the ball in his stride and struck it hard and low past the diving Main with his left foot.

Incredibly, Motherwell had taken a 3–1 lead and Hampden erupted once again. The pace of the game was frightening and yet the skill factor remained in evidence from both teams in the highest measure.

4.17

Jim McLean pulled off Ray McKinnon and brought on Billy McKinley. Dave Bowman crossed from the right and with superb timing little John O'Neil ripped into the heart of the Motherwell defence and powered a magnificent header past the struggling Maxwell. 3–2 and the game was again wide open.

Just about this point I found the time to turn to Martin Rose and say, 'Hey, this is some game we are watching.' What a masterpiece of understatement that proved to be because all sorts of drama had still to unfold before this particular match was to draw to a close.

4.18

The United team, looking like pale, strange imitations of their normal colourful selves in their all-white 'change strips' to replace their normal tangerine jerseys and black shorts, continued to surge forward. They forced another corner. Maxie came off his line and rose high to clutch it cleanly.

What a spell of pulsating football had been served up by the two competing teams. Four goals in 12 minutes – that surely is exactly what football should be all about.

I recall a conversation with the chief executive of the SFA, Mr Jim Farry. We had been discussing various footballing topics and then Jim raised himself very considerably in my estimation when he stated, 'Too many coaches and clubs forget the most important rule of all in football, and that quite simply says that the team which scores the greater number of goals shall be deemed to be the winner of the game!'

Unfortunately we all know that there has been a trend for years now for many coaches to concentrate upon the other side of the coin whereby they preach that at the start of every game each team has a draw to their credit and as long as they defend and do not lose a goal then the least that they will have by time-up is a draw. In their books that is infinitely better than a defeat. This negative attitude has been instrumental in driving countless fans away from football.

As long as top officials with attitudes similar to that of Jim Farry are in charge of our game then soccer in Scotland is in good hands.

Davie Cooper celebrates

The Motherwell players and fans cheer O'Donnell's goal

4.22

To return to the game, the United build-up became more typically composed as their passes started to find their targets with greater precision. Billy McKinlay, a very fine young player, must take some credit for this transformation because it coincided with his appearance on the field of play from the subs bench.

4.25

Luc Nijholt and Jim McInally clashed angrily and a worse flare-up was instantly averted by the timely intervention of David Syme. Jim McInally had been incensed by the solid crunching tackle with which Luc had brought down young John O'Neil.

Motherwell, with the debilitating injury to their goalie, were now playing with their backs to the wall. 'The Alamo' was an apt description for their play which I picked up from Bill Crawford who was seated just in front of our group.

4.27

Another great cut-out by the heroic Maxwell from a right-wing cross cleared the danger.

4.31

United forced yet another fruitless corner as the 'Well defenders coped admirably with everything that the Dundee side threw at them.

4.33

Maxie's right glove clutched at his left side after every time he cleared the ball up the park from his hands.

Bowman pulled at Boyd's jersey and received an elbow from Tam for his pains. The two players rounded on one another but again David Syme brought order to the proceedings and awarded the foul to the 'Well.

4.35

Young John O'Neil beat Kirk and Boyd and put in a telling cross from the right wing which Jim Griffin did well to head high over his own crossbar.

4.38

The tireless Arnott continued to harass the United defence and was pulled down by the committed Freddie Van der Hoorn. 'Coop' as usual took the free kick but this was cleared upfield.

4.39

The sharp, piercing whistling from the 'Well fans was deafening as it reached a crescendo urging David Syme to blow for time-up.

4.40

Into extra time added on for injury and, to be fair, the Maxwell injury had taken quite some time to treat.

Dougie Arnott, out on the left wing, picked up the ball and cut inside. He attempted a through pass for Phil O'Donnell who had made yet another long, lung-bursting run right through the middle. With hindsight (which is an exact science) perhaps Dougie Arnott would have done better if he had simply put his head down and made for the corner flag with the ball in order to waste a few more vital seconds. As it was, the ball ran through to Alan Main whose prodigious kick-out was headed on the first bounce by Darren Jackson, over the despairing hands of the injured Maxwell.

It was 20 seconds into injury time. The scoreline now stood at 3–3 and everyone connected to Motherwell inside Hampden Park felt completely 'gutted'. Many heads went down. With this tremendous boost to their morale, Dundee United really went flat out for the kill.

4.43

In the third minute of injury time the ball landed at the feet of the United captain, Maurice Malpas, after Jim McInally effected a tremendous dummy. Malpas had a clear sight of goal but from 12 yards he snatched at the ball and it flew high and wide of the goal. It was a gilt-edged chance squandered.

4.44

At last David Syme brought proceedings to a close. Another 30 minutes of extra time now faced the two teams who must have felt emotionally drained – each and every one of them. The same could be said of every supporter within the stadium.

4.48

Extra time got underway.

Motherwell found fresh reserves of energy from somewhere and they went at their opponents right from the kick-off. Ian Angus swung over a beauty of a cross and Main touched the ball for a corner but the referee gave a foul in favour of United.

4.52

Ian Angus forced another corner and Davie Cooper lined up to put in yet another of his tantalising specials from the right corner flag.

4.53

Alan Main, under pressure from the tall Paterson amongst others, flapped at the ball and 'Super-Sub' Stevie Kirk came in at the far post and accurately and cleanly headed the ball into Dundee United's net for what was to prove to be the winning goal in the 1991 Tennents Scottish Cup final.

4.54

Darren Jackson shot hard and low from outside the box and Maxie dived low to his right to bring off a fine save.

Nijholt had picked up Billy McKinley at the start of extra time and this was effectively stifling the United build-up.

4.57

Battling Davie Cooper headed the ball clear from inside his own six-yard box. Motherwell were revitalised and determined to give nothing more away.

5.02

There was another high ball in from the right and Maxie had to throw himself on to the feet of Jackson. He got a kick in the mouth to add to his other problems. This was actually a fine double save at a very vital stage in the game.

5.04

David Syme blew for the extra-time interval after Chris McCart had cleared the danger following a free kick which Luc Nijholt had given away when he was judged to have fouled Miodrag Krivokapic, the big Yugoslavian.

5.05

The final act got underway. Maxie's face was deeply etched with pain as he made for the ball.

5.06

A badly timed challenge just outside the Motherwell penalty box by Ian Angus nearly split young John O'Neil in two. No foul was given and play raged on.

Davie Cooper, working like a Trojan, again headed the ball clear from his own penalty box. He was the oldest player on the park and nobody had fought harder than the highly talented 'Coop'.

5.08

Davie Cooper, in the inside-right position, picked out Ian Angus with a cunning pass which allowed Angus to get his shot in on goal. Unfortunately it was from his weaker right foot and the ball went into the side-netting.

Maxie punched clear bravely under great pressure.

Luc Nijholt was shown the yellow card for a cynical tackle on Billy McKinley. David Syme's prompt action prevented any further flare-up. Davie Cooper continually switched wings, working tirelessly.

5.13

Alan Main hurried out of his box for about ten yards to meet the ball and play it back upfield. Time was rapidly running out for the Dundee team and cramp was starting to affect one or two of their players. Motherwell battled on dourly.

5.16

The ball broke out of a ruck of players in the Motherwell six-yard box and fell for Maurice Malpas who met it perfectly as he hammered it from 14 yards. The ball screamed towards the roof of the Motherwell net and it had goal written all over it. Maxwell brought off the save of the game with an instinctive, reaction touch over the bar. What a save!

Colin O'Neill

5.17

Tommy McLean brought on Colin O'Neill for Davie Cooper. Maxie punched clear but he was again fouled by John Clark.

5.19

Colin O'Neill got his first kick of the game as he cleared the ball high upfield.

5.20

Bowman challenged Colin O'Neill and the Irishman got his second kick of the game – this time from Bowman.

5.21

Still no whistle.

John Clark shot for goal from inside the box. It looked like a homer until it deflected off Jim Griffin's shin and went wide of the goal.

David Syme blew for time-up.

MOTHERWELL HAD WON THE CUP!

Dundee United were out of Europe for the first time in 15 years. Motherwell fans savoured every second of this triumphant occasion.

5.28

Tom Boyd held the Scottish Cup aloft and saluted the cheering, delirious, exhausted 'Well fans, who felt completely spent after absorbing the greatest Cup final ever played at Hampden Park.

When the final whistle was blown by David Syme amid the cheering and celebrations, I reached along to shake the hand of Tommy McClusky who was sitting two seats along from me.

Tommy, Martin Rose and I have travelled the length and breadth of the country every other week when Motherwell were playing away from home for many years now.

Tommy, who is over 70, unfortunately suffered a stroke about

Tommy Boyd holds the cup aloft and salutes the Motherwell fans

ten weeks before the final. He made a good recovery and he was allowed home about eight days before the big event.

Tommy had been determined to overcome this set-back and he said that the only thing that kept him going during those long weeks in hospital was the stubborn conviction that he would be out in time to see the 'Well in the final.

On the day of the game Martin Rose brought Tommy over to Fir Park. We had booked him in for the pre-match lunch and I arranged for him to be seated beside his old-time heroes – the seven survivors of the 1952 Cup final – who all made a fuss over Tommy. He really appreciated this.

After the meal we left in one of the dozen buses for Hampden. Tommy was on the bus which was allowed right into the reserved parking area in front of the grandstand.

He thoroughly enjoyed the game and at the end all he could say as the tears ran down his face was: 'I told you I would make it and we've won the Cup.'

That for me was the highlight of all the celebrations.

Chapter Twelve

CIVIC RECEPTION

There was an excellent turn-out of players, directors, management and backroom staff, councillors and celebrities from both the SFA and the League plus MPs and local officials at the Civic Reception in the Civic Centre on Tuesday, 28 May 1991.

An awful lot of hard work had gone into the occasion to make certain that everything went off well. Norman Turner and Anne Malloy, who are both Fir Park regulars, take great credit for the evening. The leisure department certainly played a major part in the success of this function. Even the menu had been laid out in footballing terms with a first and second half: Cup Winners Starter; Claret and Amber Entrée; onside-sweetcorn, broccoli, parisienne potatoes and boiled potatoes; Into Europe with Sweet Success; Hampden Cheeseboard; Team Spirit – Coffee, Mints and Liqueurs. The running order for the evening followed the theme:

KICK-OFF AND TEAM NEWS – Provost James Armstrong JP
MATCH REPORT – Mr W. H. Dickie
TOMMY TALKING – Tommy McLean
FINAL WHISTLE – Councillor William Wilson JP
EXTRA TIME – Motherwell District Community Choir and the Motherwell District Youth Theatre
POST-MATCH CELEBRATIONS – Disco till 1.00 a.m.

The football club really appreciated this tribute to their great Cup victory and it rounded off a spell of sustained celebrations in the town quite admirably.

Tommy McLean, Provost Armstrong, Cammy Murray and some of the team

The best thing about winning the final of the Scottish Cup is the fact that the euphoria continues from 18 May right through until the opening game of the new season in August. During the season if your team has a good result it only lasts until the next game. The old adage that 'you are only as good as your last game' is all too true in football. After the Cup final there are almost three months to bask in the reflected glory of a great result.

Chapter Thirteen

POET'S CORNER

Our Cup run seemed to encourage some fans to wax lyrical over the team's performances and here are some typical offerings. The first is anonymous:

MOTHERWELL 4 CELTIC 2

Now the press along with Andy Gray
Said we'd never cope with Elliot and McStay
And when we gave them a goal of a start
They said the 'Well would fall apart

But did we buckle? not the slightest bit
Wee Dougie's equaliser was brilliantly hit
Then Celtic scored to lead once again
The know-alls said we'd had it then

But they forgot we're men of steel
A curse to Smiler one Billy McNeil
From Arnott's head the ball just flew
Past Bonnar's hands, now it was 2–2

Andy Gray and the rest still tipped Celts to win
When Colin O'Neill stuck one on their chin
From 40 yards out he struck that ball
Poor Paddy Bonnar had no chance at all

Stevie Kirk expresses his delight after beating Bonnar
(Picture: Craig Halkett)

Could Celtic come back from off the floor
Or would the dossers get number four
As on to the park came our super sub
The Parkhead noses he didn't half rub

When the whistle blew the fans stayed to cheer
And Big Billy quickly seemed to disappear
He must have been under a helluva stress
As he didn't come out to talk to the press

We'd no Davie Cooper nor Bobby Russell
But their deputies gave plenty hustle and bustle
So just let me say it's not meant as a craw
It's easy when you know where to put the baw

The second is a bit longer and it was composed by Mrs Sutherland for her ten-year-old nephew. She passed it on to the club and I am pleased to include it in this book which is as much a tribute to our loyal fans as it is to the team!

THE SCOTTISH CUP FINAL
18 MAY 1991
DUNDEE UNITED 3 MOTHERWELL 4

For weeks excitement's been buzzing roon
Cup final fever had hit oor toon
Shop windows were dressed as never before
With claret and amber and best wishes galore.

The fans they all gathered from far and near
To give their support to our Team of the Year
At last it came the magic day
To Hampden Park we're on our way

That glorious moment, will we ever forget?
Iain Ferguson headed our first goal into the net
The crowd was ecstatic, they gave out a roar
'Come on, boys, please give us some more'

The second half started the 'Well one goal up
We're in with a chance of winning the Cup
To our great disappointment and our surprise
Bowman 'slipped' one in to equalise

A job well done! Kirkie and Fergie enjoy the moment

Our goal number two went in like a dream
From young Phil O'Donnell his first for his team
A grounder from Ian Angus made the fans dance with glee
Dundee United one, Motherwell three.

Thing's were really looking swell
The Cup's on its way to Motherwell
Then a header from O'Neil, that came out of the blue
Giving Dundee United a total of two

'Come on now, lads, please keep the heid
You know you're still one goal in the lead'
But alas with only seconds to go
Jackson scored with cries of 'Oh No!'

Into extra time now, lads, do not sway
Your fans are with you every inch of the way
In the dugout Tommy was gie agitated
For this was the day all his life he had waited

141

In goal 'Hero Ally' nursed his side in great pain
Oh Lord! Would our hearts be able to take the strain?
On comes 'Psycho' midst cheers galore
Could he do something to up our score?

A magnificent header from Stevie Kirk
Was the final goal that did the trick
The roar from the crowd the 'Super Sub' was given
Surely must have been heard in heaven

The minutes ticked by, the fans held their breath
They knew that their team would fight to the death
At last! At last! The final whistle blew
Oh Motherwell, your dream has come true

'Congratulations' to Motherwell
Our pounding hearts with pride did swell
You've won the Cup, oh! What a team
'Well done, lads' we all did scream.

Cathie Sutherland
Wishaw

And yet another offering.

'OWED' TO THE 'WELL

I woke up at seven, as I couldn't sleep,
I'll go for a run and see the sheep.
When coming up the braes to my surprise,
Sitting in the fields were five magpies.

Five's for silver, this must be fate,
I'll spring up the road and phone the mate.
He couldn't sleep so he was up,
'Yer right wee man, we'll lift the Cup.'

We went to Motherwell, the girls and I,
Just passing time and feeling so high.
The town was busy, we had to clamber,
Through a veritable 'sea' of claret and amber.

142

We set off for Hampden at one o'clock,
Our resolve was steady, solid as a rock.
We'll win this Cup there is not a doubt,
Then on to the terracing, 'The 'Well' was the shout.

The game had just started, I was standing with pride,
The ball's in the net, thank Gawd it's offside.
A Van de Hoorn shot which was better than most,
Fortunately for us, came back off the post.

We started to attack, the ball was chipped through,
A Ferguson flick and Griffin's cross was true.
As Fergie rose high, his head was set,
To bullet the ball into the back of the net.

At half time we're leading and looking the part,
Then a collision with Maxie, right at the start.
As he came for the ball, his innards sank,
He bounced off John Clark, the human tank.

The fray was restarted and United replied,
A blooter from Bowman went in unspied.
Poor Ally was injured, he just couldn't dive,
His vision was doubled, he felt barely alive.

We went right up the park and won a free kick,
Their defence was not ready, Cooper took it quick.
Big Craig jumped high in an effort to win,
It broke to young Phil who nodded it in.

The fans were ecstatic and were extolling the 'Well,
When the ball was chipped forward for Kirk to excel.
He set up Ian Angus who arriving like a train,
Skelped a scorcher past the despairing Main.

United redoubled their efforts and more,
They stormed up the park determined to score.
Attack after attack, their intentions were real,
Then a Bowman cross was headed in by O'Neil.

With our backs to the wall and time to spend,
We tried to hold out in defence to the end.
One minute of play until the whistle would sound,
Then a sickening blow smashed us back to the ground.

A rocket from Main went right up the park,
The Motherwell defence were unsure who to mark.
The ball soared onwards and an unlucky bounce,
Was spotted by Jackson who was ready to pounce.

The ball was past Maxie, it was their goal,
Their fans were delirious, their Cup dreams were whole.
Their celebrations were jubilant, depression was mine,
As the final whistle blew, hailing extra-time.

We started again and moved right into attack,
Their defence was poor, their marking slack.
A deep cross to Kirk whose header net-bound,
Brought a one-handed save from a keeper so sound.

That was the beginning as more was to follow,
A corner from Cooper found Main's hands were hollow.
The ball's flight continued and to United's dismay,
The header from Kirk was IN all the way.

The nerves were now jangling – blow your whistle, ref,
Ignoring our pleas, Syme appeared to be quite deaf.
A rocket from Malpas was going in, under the bar,
When touched over by Maxie, our goalkeeper star.

The whistle was blown, the game is now over,
The noise is fantastic, the fans are in clover.
They're jumping, they're hugging, they're singing their joys,
Appreciating the performance from the Motherwell boys.

The Cup is collected and being shown to the fans,
And draped on the Cup are claret and amber bands.
My feelings are inexplicable and tongue can not tell,
My elation that day when following the 'Well.

Douglas Bennett

The fans gather at Fir Park for the return of their team

Nijholt, Arnott and Boyd take their bow

Chapter Fourteen

WHAT THE PAPERS SAID

The *Motherwell Times*, 11 May 1991:

CUP FEVER HITS TOWN
by
Allan McIntyre

All roads will lead to Hampden on Saturday when Motherwell tackle Dundee United in their quest for Scottish Cup glory.

The town has been buzzing with excitement since Tommy McLean's men dumped Celtic in a semi-final replay on 9 April, and the build-up reached fever pitch this week.

It has been billed as the family final with the team's faithful followers joined on Saturday by wives, girlfriends, kids, grannies, aunts and uncles who are all going along to cheer the 'Well.

Those who remember the excitement of Motherwell winning the Scottish Cup in 1952 proudly recall being at Hampden on that April day when 136,304 fans watched Motherwell beat Dundee 4−0.

There will be less at Hampden on Saturday − capacity crowd now 64,000 − but no one wants to miss out on seeing their side lift the national trophy and the final looks certain to be a sell-out.

This is Motherwell's first major final since their victory 39 years ago and the town will be deserted. It's a boom day for coach hirers with every available bus in Lanarkshire in use on Saturday.

The response when tickets went on sale at Fir Park more than a week ago was tremendous and the club has now sold its allocation of 22,500 ground tickets. Only tickets available at Fir Park are for the family section.

Motherwell secretary Alan Dick has been inundated with postal requests and not just from Scotland. Mail has been flooding in from England and overseas.

Anyone with the slightest Motherwell connection wants to be at Hampden on Saturday and that includes many people from the town now living abroad.

Some of those who are making the special journey back include David Bill, who stays in California, George Simonetti, who is coming from Italy, and Motherwell couple Alan and Val Caldwell now living in Melbourne.

Motherwell fan Ian Skelly is interrupting a holiday in Florida to return for the final and former Motherwell director Jim Hepburn is flying over from California to see it.

And like all of them the *Motherwell Times* wishes Motherwell manager Tommy McLean and his players the best of luck in the final.

We'll be there backing you and waiting to join in the celebrations at the final whistle.

The *Motherwell Times*:

TOM WINS BATTLE FOR FINAL SPOT
by
Allan McIntyre

Bobby Russell was ruled out of Motherwell's Scottish Cup squad earlier in the week when he failed in his battle to get over a knee injury.

But one player who has won the fitness fight is captain Tom Boyd, and he looks certain to play in what will be his final match for Motherwell at Hampden on Saturday.

Tom limped off during the semi-final replay against Celtic and it looked then as if that would be his last match for the club.

He gave what appeared then to be a farewell wave to the Motherwell fans as he hobbled along the touchline, but the Scottish international is set to make a dramatic first-team return in the Scottish Cup final.

Robert Russell, who missed the final due to injury

On his injury, Tom said: 'I thought at the time that the injury was worse and that was my last game for Motherwell. But I have now played in a couple of reserve games and came through them all right. It would be great to finish here by helping Motherwell to win the Scottish Cup.'

And on his chances of collecting a winner's medal before heading off to a new club, Tom said: 'Now we have just one more team to beat. We won't have any fears going into the final. We have got to go into it optimistic. We are going in confident that we have the players with the ability to win the game.'

There are still huge question marks over where the 25-year-old defender will end up but that won't be decided until the final is over. On the move, Tom added: 'I have just tried to keep my mind on the Cup and as far as moving is concerned, that will come later.'

One player still battling to make it to the final is midfield power-house Colin O'Neill.

The Irishman has been struggling to get over a knee injury but had spells in two reserve games last Thursday and Saturday. And a special closed-door match was arranged on Tuesday to test his fitness.

It was O'Neill's wonder third goal that clinched the tie against Celtic, and he said: 'That was the best moment of my life. But if it hadn't gone in I would have been in bother for not playing the ball wide.

'The important thing for me now is to hope that I will be fit and make it into the manager's team.'

Motherwell supporters are hoping that their two-goal semi-final hero, Dougie Arnott, shows the same form on his return to Hampden.

He has already been in two Scottish Cup finals at amateur and junior levels. Both games ended in disappointment for Dougie, Motherwell Miners losing 2–1 and Pollock beaten 3–2.

But he is looking for a change of fortune on Saturday and said: 'I didn't like the feeling after the last two finals so I will be looking for a third time lucky and a victory to celebrate.

'It was tremendous scoring my first goals at Hampden against Celtic in the semi-final. It's great getting to the final, especially the way we won the replay after the start Celtic made to it. But what about that fluke by Colin O'Neill for the third?'

Local boy Dougie has lots of relatives travelling up from England for the match as his mother comes from Liverpool and his home town of Carluke will be giving him their full support.

The player Motherwell fans want to see on the substitutes' bench is Steve Kirk. He has been something of a lucky mascot for the Steelmen so far, coming on as substitute to score against Aberdeen, Falkirk and Celtic and scoring one of the penalties in the spotkick win over Morton.

Latest youngster to make an impact on the side is 19-year-old Phil O'Donnell, who was another of the stars in the 4–2 win over Celtic.

And on his breakthrough the midfielder said: 'It's great and I am loving it.

'At the start of the season I was hoping to get into the squad and get the odd game in the first team.

'Playing in the semi-final at Hampden was just terrific. What an atmosphere and to beat Celtic was great.

'If selected for the final it would be a dream come true. We all think we can win the Cup.'

*Colin O'Neill immediately after scoring the greatest goal of his life
(Picture: Craig Halkett, courtesy of the* Daily Record)

Motherwell fans know they are in safe hands with Alastair Maxwell, now Scotland's third choice keeper.

His save of the season was in the semi-final when Motherwell were leading 3–2 and Paul McStay made his way into the box.

And on the save, he said: 'If Celtic had scored then they could have taken it from there. To be honest it's probably the most vital save I have made in my career.

'He struck it really well but I got a good hand to it. The ball just stuck on the ground but Luc was there to clear.'

And what a season it will be for Dutchman Luc Nijholt, who joined the club last August. He broke his leg in a League match against Celtic in January but was back to his best to star in the semi-final matches.

On the Cup run, he said: 'It's been a good season for me apart from my leg break.

'For me the semi-final was special. The atmosphere was brilliant and I am now looking forward to the final.

'Hopefully we will now win the Cup and take Motherwell into Europe for the first time.'

Motherwell are the only side in the Premier League who have not played in a European tournament, but the loyal Fir Park supporters are already checking out their passports for next season.

The *Motherwell Times*, 16 May 1991:

THE FINAL SHOWDOWN
TOMMY'S TROOPS GUNNING FOR HAMPDEN GLORY

Motherwell players have the chance to write their names into the history books on Saturday – and give the club its first taste of European football.

Boss Tommy McLean says there is no reason why his club cannot win its first major honour in 39 years. And there are few, if any, Lanarkshire football fans who will disagree.

Motherwell have been the shock team in this season's Tennents Scottish Cup – given little chance when faced with a trip to Pittodrie against the holders and once again written off as they went in to tackle Celtic in a semi-final replay.

But the players have shown their grit and determination and are just 90 minutes away from emulating the Motherwell team of 1952.

Tommy McLean is approaching Saturday's match in a positive mood, and says: 'I am going into it optimistic and hopeful. I don't see any reason why we should not be. We have already beaten Aberdeen and Celtic and had the recent victory over Rangers. We cannot be anything but optimistic.

'But having said that, it won't just happen. It has to be achieved. The players have to approach this in the same manner as they did these other games. Any passengers will let the team down badly.

'They have got to battle and work hard for each other.'

The 'Well boss takes his squad of 18 players to Irvine today (Thursday) for their final preparations.

Jamie Dolan, who was in the squad but missed out on the big day

And he summed up just how important the match will be to his men: 'A Cup final is there to be enjoyed. It's a gala occasion and I want them to savour every minute of it.

'But they are not just there to get involved in all the off-the-field stuff. They have to concentrate.

'They are just 90 minutes away from being the first players to take Motherwell into European football. That has to be their drive and ambition.'

Tommy is up against brother Jim's Dundee United – and Motherwell fans will be hoping their opponents' Scottish Cup final jinx continues.

United go into Saturday's match knowing that they have lost in all of their five appearances in the national final, four times in the past ten years.

It may have taken Motherwell a long time to return to Hampden in a Scottish Cup final but their fans are certain that 1991 is once again their year for Hampden glory.

Ally Maxwell, the *hero of the final*

Scotland On Sunday, 19 May 1991:

MAXWELL'S FINAL ACT OF COURAGE
by
Kevin McCarra

Motherwell won the Scottish Cup because they are the experts in adversity. The rudiments of glamour may now have arrived at Fir Park but the side remember humbler days and possess sound instincts when called upon to struggle.

Nothing was allowed to shake their calm belief in their right to collect the trophy this season. Motherwell were steadfastly unimpressed as their opponents smoothly outplayed them for the opening half hour. After they had gone into the lead, all their hopes seemed to have been shattered by the moment early in the second half when goalkeeper Ally Maxwell suffered an agonising rib injury.

153

With a display of stark courage the goalkeeper refused to succumb to his own pain. The impairment to his performance allowed United to overhaul a 3–1 deficit and push the match into extra time. All the same Maxwell's valour was not in vain.

Once substitute Steve Kirk had provided one of his patented Cup-tie sensations with a goal in 94 minutes, it became obvious that the scoreline had changed shape for the last time. Maxwell's astounding save from a Maurice Malpas drive three minutes from the end was an unforgettable gesture of defiance.

As always there are numbers to be juggled. Motherwell collected the Cup once again after a gap of 39 years. There must also be mention of United's sixth failure to win in the final. Motherwell now enter Europe for the first time in their history, but United will be absent from the arena for the first time since 1976.

It is better, however, for their fans to dwell on the nobility of the final seconds of this thrilling contest. With the last kick of the match John Clark shot from close in directly in front of the target. His drive was deflected wide and referee David Syme signalled the end of the match. The United defender had inflicted the Motherwell goalkeeper's injury, but now he reached forward spontaneously to embrace Maxwell. His grief at losing could wait.

This final will accordingly be remembered as a ragged classic. It refused to conform to the audience's expectations, or to the managers' intentions. At the end it was scarcely recognisable as the same game which had begun so methodically two and a half hours earlier.

With the brothers McLean in control there was always bound to be evidence of mental exertion. With a cast of entirely familiar faces they endeavoured to put one another in novel difficulties. Tommy McLean's Motherwell had Tom Boyd operating in the heart of defence and centre-back Chris McCart wide on the right.

Jim McLean's slightly revamped United had Duncan Ferguson operating in a new role just behind the attack. With so much tactical complexity the formations looked like the probable answer to a question concerning the theory of relativity.

The initial outcome of it all, however, was simplicity itself. Dundee United were governing the play from the opening moments and might have been two up in seven minutes. Two minutes into the game Jim McInally sent Hamish French away to stroke a shot home. The referee, though, had detected a hint of offside, and chalked it off. Then, a free kick was touched sideways to Freddie van der Hoorn 25 yards out. His firm precise shot struck the inside of one post and ran across the line before eventually going behind.

Motherwell were lethal when the chance to threaten at last presented itself. In 32 minutes a Jim Griffin cross, which took a slight deflection, came to Iain Ferguson, and the former Dundee United striker headed firmly home. Maxwell collapsed under a legal challenge by Clark in 50 minutes. He was in obvious agony thereafter, a tremor of pain shooting through his body each time he kicked out. After 56 minutes he was unable to move with his normal ease and a 25-yard drive from Dave Bowman flew past him.

Three minutes later Motherwell restored their lead. Davie Cooper pumped in a free kick and Craig Paterson leaped to knock the ball across for teenager Phil O'Donnell to lunge and head into the net.

When Kirk laid the ball back for Ian Angus to score with a precise 20-yard drive after 65 minutes Motherwell seemed secure. United, however, fought back furiously and were aided by Maxwell's difficulties. Substitute John O'Neil headed home a Bowman cross in 67 minutes. Then, in the final moments of normal time Darren Jackson chased a kickout and nodded the ball over the advancing goalkeeper.

Four minutes into extra time Davie Cooper's corner was knocked on and Kirk rose to head the winning goal at the back post. It was a fitting conclusion. He had started it all with his club's decisive strike at Pittodrie in the third round and now he had steered them through to its final glory.

The Glasgow *Evening Times*, 20 May 1991:

A CRIME OF PASSION
by
Alan Davidson

The Cup finalists combined to encapsulate the greatest dilemma facing Scottish football as it approaches the 21st century.

Does the old business continue to rely on the combination of naive enthusiasm, aggression and skill that turned the confrontation between Motherwell and Dundee United into one of the most exciting Hampden finals seen in almost 120 years?

Or should it try to attain the technical standards of Europe's leading clubs at the risk of putting the public to sleep without the need of a doctor's prescription?

A poll of the 58,000 at Hampden and the million watching on live TV would certainly return only one verdict.

And that would be overwhelmingly in favour of the game we know and love when it is played with such a breathtaking level of passion.

Whatever its frailties, and there are many, Scottish football still has a lot to offer to the paying public. Packaged as it was by Motherwell and United, it is close to irresistible.

Bertie Auld, as enthralled as the rest of us as he sat in the stand watching a true classic unfold, knows all about the conflicting demands of the Scottish and European versions of the game.

But the man who was one of the most potent members of Celtic's European Cup winning side of 1967 is in no doubt about the priorities, and they centre on the excitement provided by the teams.

'I WOULD PAY GOOD MONEY EVERY WEEK TO WATCH A MATCH LIKE THAT, AND I THINK EVERY FOOTBALL-MINDED PERSON IN THE COUNTRY WOULD AGREE,' AULD SAID.

There are times when you wonder if it is worth crossing the road to see a game – even at the supposedly highest level – but when two Scottish teams are prepared to give what the players of Motherwell and United did then it restores the faith.

'At its best, and that is what we saw on Saturday, our game stands comparison with anything on offer elsewhere.

'It was a pure joy to watch, and it has had everyone talking. Even women and wee girls who normally wouldn't think about football loved it.

'Surely that is what the game is about – attracting people who otherwise wouldn't be interested.

'It was an outstanding advert for Scottish football, especially when you compare it to what was on offer in the English Cup final. Maybe it isn't the kind of game that is geared to success in Europe, but does that really matter?' Auld asked.

It's a long time since Rangers won the Scottish Cup, but three of their former players received gold medals in 1991

'First and foremost you must give your own public what they want, and nobody left Hampden feeling short-changed.'

Of course, if you live in Lanarkshire or Dundee, the fact that Motherwell emerged with the trophy courtesy of a 4–3 win after extra time isn't irrelevant.

LIKEWISE THEIR ULTIMATE TRIUMPH WAS TOTALLY DESERVED IF ONLY FOR THE SEEMINGLY BOTTOMLESS WELL OF DESIRE AND RAW COURAGE THEY SHOWED.

But – at the risk of dredging up an ancient cliché – football won at Hampden as the teams set about one another, completely committed but still managing to embrace the spirit of sport.

Every one of the 26 players who took part can be proud of his contribution to an outstanding afternoon of sheer entertainment that will live for all time in the memories of those who watched.

Basically, it was great fun as Motherwell went ahead in a comparatively ordinary first half through an Iain Ferguson header.

It was all a touch tentative in these opening 45 minutes, and nothing on offer prepared us for a colossal second half.

The final ebbed and flowed.

United equalised through Dave Bowman, Motherwell went 3–1 ahead via outstanding goals from Philip O'Donnell and Ian Angus, only for the Tannadice side to pull one back with a header by substitute John O'Neil and an equaliser in the final minute of normal time through Darren Jackson.

At that stage the clever money was on United. Their morale and confidence had soared, and in Ally Maxwell they were taking on a goalkeeper whose broken ribs and damaged stomach muscles should have had him in hospital rather than between the posts.

Hospital is where he ended up later.

But not before continuing to provide a performance of immense courage as his team-mates tried to protect him from another dose of the pain inflicted when John Clark – who would be entitled to step into a ring with Mike Tyson – careered into him early in the second half.

Stevie Kirk, who had started it all with a last minute winner against Aberdeen at Pittodrie in January, headed what proved to be the decisive goal in the first half of extra time.

IT SEEMED THE WHOLE OF MOTHERWELL CELE-BRATED, AND NOW THEY HAVE EUROPEAN FOOTBALL TO LOOK FORWARD TO IN THE CUP WINNERS' CUP NEXT SEASON.

But will the fans turn up consistently in numbers to provide the backing they were prepared to give on Saturday?

Auld hopes so, and said: 'I think Motherwell, and United as well, have shown they deserve much bigger supports than they have been enjoying.

'Their people owe that to them after the way in which they were entertained in the final.

'Honestly, I believe Motherwell can really benefit from this success. I remember the lift everyone at Celtic got after we beat Dunfermline in the 1965 Scottish Cup final.

'That was a similar type of game. It went one way and then the other before Billy McNeill won the Cup for us late on.

'We all felt we could take on anyone after that, and went on to prove the confidence wasn't misplaced by winning the European Cup two years later.

'Motherwell should be equally happy after what they put into that match.

'They are in Europe now, and if they can show the enthusiasm and will that drove them to their win then there's no reason why they shouldn't have a decent European run.'

In the *Evening Times* 'SHOOT AT TRAYNOR', the following three letters appeared on Monday, 22 May 1991:

WHO NEEDS OLD FIRM?

The match that was dubbed 'The Family Final' certainly lived up to expectations as Motherwell and Dundee United gave everyone full value in excitement and goals.

Indeed, the great pity was that there had to be a loser on such a great occasion.

It was a great joy to watch coachloads of supporters from Motherwell and Dundee turn up at Hampden and we had mums and dads and their children mingling with rival supporters in good spirits and obvious enjoyment.

We also had a real hero of the hour in Motherwell keeper Alastair Maxwell playing on with a severe stomach injury.

Scottish football was considerably enhanced, as it turned out, by the fact that Motherwell and Dundee United reached the Scottish Cup final. We could do with many more occasions like this.

Compare this to an 'Old Firm' final and the sight of supporters singing sectarian songs at each other with obvious hatred on their faces and we can only be thankful that teams from the provinces do reach finals sometimes.

Motherwell and Dundee United are to be congratulated on serving up a game that was as exciting as any Cup final we have witnessed in previous years, and it was all in the best possible traditions of Scottish football.

JAMES M. GIBSON

CLASSIC FINAL

The Motherwell–Dundee United Scottish Cup final was the greatest match I have ever had the privilege to watch.

*O'Neill, Maxwell and Cooper on one of their regular visits to their fans
in hospital*

We can't thank both clubs enough for serving up a magnificent feast of fast attacking football and it was all played in a magnificent spirit. It was a great final, unsurpassed in modern times.

Every goal was a classic, even the one which was disallowed, and the friendly spirit of the two sets of supporters was a credit to Motherwell and Dundee.

Personally, I was particularly impressed with Alastair Maxwell for the courage he showed in carrying on despite the fact that he was in obvious pain. He has to be the bravest goalkeeper in Britain.

It was also good to see the way United players congratulated their opponents at the end of extra-time.

JAMES HAROLD

WELL EARNED

Everyone tried to play down the Scottish Cup final just because Rangers and Celtic weren't involved, but in the end all the detractors were left with egg on their face.

We were led to believe that the final would be nothing more than a brotherly kick-about, but we now know different.

Seven goals, plenty of excitement and two teams going about their business without the sort of tension that is experienced at 'Old Firm' matches. It was wonderful stuff.

Motherwell, in the end, deserved to win the Cup and I am a Dundee United fan. After all, the Lanarkshire side did have to dispose of both Aberdeen and Celtic to get there.

Celtic thought that it was their right to be in the final after having defeated Rangers, but Motherwell re-wrote the script brilliantly, although I'm just sorry it wasn't to be United's day.

Still, we'll be there again next year.

JENNIFER THOMSON

Chapter Fifteen

A SOUR NOTE

Just over a month after David Syme blew the final whistle at Hampden to bring the season to an end the SFA dealt severely with four Dundee United players who had been booked by the referee *after* the game had ended.

Darren Jackson, John Clark, Jim McInally and Freddie Van der Hoorn were uncompromisingly 'red carded' in the tunnel by David Syme for 'foul and abusive language'. They were obviously upset at losing but it would seem that they temporarily lost their discipline after the game and made the mistake of challenging Mr Syme.

With the automatic five penalty points which go along with a red card this meant that Dundee United were without the services of all four players at the start of season 1991/92. Darren Jackson missed one game, John Clark and Jim McInally both missed two games and Freddie Van der Hoorn missed out on three games. In addition, £12,000 of Cup final bonus payments were withheld from Dundee United.

This is a sad picture to present to the public, particularly when you consider the excellent spirit in which the whole game was played. A certain degree of sympathy will be felt by many for the four offenders but the authority of the referee must at all times be upheld and, even taking into consideration the strong feelings of disappointment which must have been welling up inside every United player, it is impossible to condone the behaviour of the four players who were booked.

David Syme was probably the single main reason for this game being the great spectacle it turned out to be. His use of the 'advantage rule', his domination of the match and the manner in which be brooked no questioning of his authority, plus the understanding way in which he separated the malicious from the accidental and over-enthusiastic, were excellent examples to any aspiring referee.

The game flowed from one end to another with none of those niggling stoppages which all too often spoil matches for the viewing public when controlled by officials who fail to realise that the best matches are those in which the spectators are barely aware of the presence of the referee. In attempting to impose their authority on a game too many referees finish up being the centrepiece of the game.

David Syme gets my vote as being the finest referee that I saw in season 1990/91 and that is NOT simply because my team lifted the Cup. He did make mistakes during the 120 minutes but they were honest mistakes and very few in number. I remember an old fan who stated, 'If a referee was perfect and applied the rules 100 per cent without using his common sense, games wouldn't be worth watching.' David Syme did football a great service on 18 May 1991 with his overall performance. Sadly, the conduct of the offending four after the game did nothing for the sport.

Chapter Sixteen

INTO EUROPE

The most far-reaching effect of Motherwell's Scottish Cup victory is without doubt the fact that for the very first time they will be competing in a European tournament. The draw paired them with Katowice of Poland and while this is a little bit disappointing it will do for starters.

Katowice is in the heart of the Silesian coalfields and it is certainly not the place that 'Well fans would have chosen for their European baptism. On the brighter side the Polish team were seeded in 16th position in the Cup draw, so there were another 15 teams which could have made our progress more difficult.

Alan Dick, the club secretary, suddenly finds himself engulfed in a mountain of paperwork as UEFA send him a series of directives and questionnaires. By the time he has complied with the former and replied to the latter, there will be very little that UEFA do not know about Motherwell FC.

The standing areas behind both goals will only be allowed to fill 70 per cent of their capacity during games. Players' jerseys must carry numbers which comply with the sizes laid down by UEFA. The Motorola logo must not exceed 32 square inches. Lighting at Fir Park must attain UEFA minimum standards for brightness. The dimensions of the playing surface must be submitted before any match can take place.

All very time-consuming but Alan will cope without any problem. The fans have looked on jealously from the side lines for many years as other teams enjoyed the limelight and excitement

The victors – into Europe

of European football; now for the first time Motherwell can do likewise. Now that the opportunity presents itself there is bound to be a capacity crowd at the opening game against Katowice at Fir Park, and although it is not the most accessible place on the continent, 'Well fans will devise ways and means of getting to Katowice. They are sure to enjoy and savour the occasion to the full!

One thing in our favour is the fact that Tommy McLean has a wealth of European experience under his belt and indeed he can boast a European Cup Winners Cup medal (the gold variety) to his credit. He could well be better placed than most to cope with the away leg. Anyone who can manage a team which can hold the multi-million pound Rangers side at Ibrox to a series of very tight results should have the expertise to handle the away leg in Poland.

Some people were a bit disappointed with the draw and bemoan the fact it is rather depressing in the coalfields of Katowice. On the brighter side they have at least managed to avoid Tel Boy's Spurs and Fergie's Man Utd. Imagine winning your way into Europe and being drawn to play within the United Kingdom!

Dixie Deans, the former Motherwell striker, now runs a pub in Carluke and he has organised a coach to travel to Poland for the first game in Katowice. His patrons have added a nice wee touch by gathering an assortment of 'luxury' goods such as tins of soup, beans and other delicacies plus a large number of kiddies' toys. Dixie said that he was trying to brighten up the lives of the locals over there. Who knows, perhaps some well-meaning Poles will reciprocate after reading about Dalzell and Ravenscraig and when they come over here they might distribute sauerkraut and potatoes to the community in Lanarkshire!

Back at Fir Park there has been a massive demand for season tickets and with the new East stand completed, the ground has received its biggest face lift for over 30 years. There is a new spirit of optimism afoot in the community and a feeling that 'the sleeping giant' has awakened at long last. Motherwell Football Club could be at the start of a new era. The club has tasted success and they are now hungry for more – much, much more!

Chapter Seventeen

BACK TO THE BAND

Motherwell have decided to revert back to the traditional claret band across the front of their jerseys. Tommy McLean is a bit of a traditionalist and he thought that this would be an improvement on previous designs. This would mean a change from their Cup-winning strip but – who knows? – perhaps the new top will feature among the honours in the near future.

By the way, it is an interesting thought that the formation and selection of the Cup final team was completely unique. That was the first and last time that those 13 players were to play in that particular grouping. Colin O'Neill, for example, is an unusual sight on the substitutes bench. Tom Boyd is now with Chelsea so there is no way that Tommy McLean can ever pick the same 13 players to play as a team again.

It was back in 1913 that Motherwell first adopted the claret and amber colours of Lord Hamilton of Dalzell. They discarded their blue tops and played in claret jerseys with cuffs and collars in amber. The band of claret on an amber jersey came in the Twenties.

In those days the band was fully six inches broad and went right round the whole jersey. Shorts were white. That was the standard attire for Motherwell for many years. Bobby Howitt opted for all amber (including the shorts) and claret trim with no band but this was not popular.

When Ian St John became manager he brought back the band but in a competition which he threw open to the fans he asked them to design a new Motherwell outfit. The winning entry which was adopted had claret shorts and a diagonal band across the front of the jersey.

Willie McLean dispensed with the St John strip and used the top in all amber with three narrow lines on the outside of the arms. Then, in 1978, when Rodger Hynd took over, he went for amber tops with claret shorts and two narrow vertical bands from shoulder to waist on the left-hand side of the jersey.

After relegation, Ally McLeod found it difficult to get a company to supply Motherwell with jerseys but eventually he managed to persuade the company which supplied Nottingham Forest with their yellow outfits, trimmed with blue, to supply Motherwell as well. This entailed using claret trim on the all-yellow outfits and having MFC embroidered on the front. It was a most insipid outfit. Under David Hay, Motherwell actually wore the same strip as Bradford City who play in claret and gold. The broad vertical bands were never really popular, though, and a couple of years later we returned to the more traditional 'Well band under Jock Wallace.

Tommy McLean has experimented with various more modern designs but he has finally opted for tradition and Motherwell will be playing in Europe in their traditional band. The only change from the past seven years will be the name of the new team sponsors – Motorola – on the claret band.

Another spin-off from the club's recent success was the approach by Tartan Sportswear Ltd of Glasgow to see whether or not we would like to have a Motherwell tartan produced. Several different designs were submitted and I presented them to the board of directors who made their choice.

Tartan Sportswear tried valiantly to have the newly registered tartan available in time for the Cup final but due to circumstances outwith their control they failed, narrowly, to have the tartan in production for 18 May. It is now available and I would predict that it will prove to be very popular with the fans. As well as the traditional Highland dresswear, there will be a wide range of tartan scarves, ties, caps, trews and rugby tops with tartan trim.

Orders have already been placed by some fans who are getting married and who have decided to wear the full Highland regalia in Motherwell tartan. There will be no shortage of articles to purchase in the Motherwell souvenir shops prior to Christmas this year and I would be surprised if the tartan is not in great demand.

Yet another spin-off for Motherwell has been the 400 per cent increase in the uptake of season tickets for 1991/92 season. The office staff have been inundated as fans flooded in to take advantage of the ten per cent price reduction for tickets purchased before the end of June.

Young Phil O'Donnell, seen here in action against Falkirk. Phil is a product of Tommy McLean's youth policy

Chapter Eighteen

A BOYS' GAME

'Boys don't win you anything' is a saying often quoted in football's managerial circles. The truth of it has been borne out on countless occasions down through the years.

Probably the best way to underline the statement would be to have a look at the most talented squad of players ever to be brought together at Fir Park. I refer of course to 'The Ancell Babes'. They had in their midst players of prodigious talent and skill: Ian St John, Willie Hunter, Pat Quinn, Andy Weir, Bobby Roberts, Billy and Sammy Reid, Bert McCann, Matt Thomson, Charlie Aitken, John Martis, etc.

I have never before or since seen more attractive football played by any other team in claret and amber. When they were on song, they were a real joy to behold and on their day they could, and did, meet and beat the finest teams in the land.

If you take Charlie Aitken out of the list of 'Ancell Babes' then their average age when they played together would be around 19! As I said earlier, they were dynamic, exciting, lethal but they were also young and inexperienced and, to be honest, a bit unpredictable and inconsistent at times. That is why the 'Ancell Babes' never won a trophy for Motherwell. They came close and were beaten in a semi-final against Clyde but they never won anything.

Ian St John reckons that if the Motherwell directors of that era had shown a little bit of belief in their manager and enabled him to hold on to his players instead of selling so many of them, Motherwell, and not Celtic, could have been the team of the

Sixties. All that was lacking in the 'Ancell Babes' was maturity. There were simply too many players with great potential or ability but sadly they were too young to have been 'over the course'.

Having said that, every football manager worth his salt must have a youth policy. The sensible managers nurse their young players along, although there is always the really exceptional youngster who simply can't be held back and who proves to one and all that he is good enough at a very early age. Tommy Boyd fell into that category and so does Phil O'Donnell. Tommy seized his opportunity and played so well he couldn't be left out. Young Phil O'Donnell looks set to do exactly the same as his former team captain.

Bobby Jenks was brought in by Tommy McLean to organise Motherwell's youth policy. Bobby has teams playing at every age level every week during their season, from Under-11s to Under-18s. They all play under the banner of Motherwell Boys' Club.

Obviously the better players are tied to the club as 'S' form signings but since boys develop at differing stages and ages the door is never closed on any lad. They are closely monitored and their progress or lack of it duly noted. Very often it is the late developer who turns out to be the best prospect at the end of the day.

Bobby Jenks does a tremendous job as youth development officer and chief scout. He is also used extensively to 'suss out' the opposition and the reports he gives on his spying missions can prove invaluable on occasions. This of course is the modern trend and Bobby Jenks fulfils the function admirably.

Phil O'Donnell is the 1991 'success story' as far as the Motherwell youth policy is concerned. He has played for some years with the Boys' Club and he won an Under-18 Scottish Amateur Cup Winners medal almost exactly one year to the day before he won his Scottish Cup Winners medal with the big team.

Bobby's team lifted the Under-18s Scottish Amateur Cup for the second year in a row when Motherwell Boys' Club beat Partick Thistle Boys' Club only a few days after the big team's triumph against Dundee United. At the end of 1990/91, Bobby Jenks' Under-18 squad had only lost about four matches in two full seasons and in that time they had lifted every honour available to them (many of the tournaments were won twice in a row). This tremendous record is better than that of any other Under-18 team

Some of the team relax after the Celtic replay

in the country and it is one of which Bobby Jenks can be justifiably proud.

It costs an awful lot of money to run about ten teams each week. It can also be very time-consuming. But when a player such as Phil O'Donnell comes through the ranks he sets a great example for every other boy involved in the Motherwell youth set-up.

To return to the earlier theme of this chapter, Tommy McLean has not fallen into the trap of having to depend upon a team of young and inexperienced players. He has blended astutely some of his better young players with some very experienced professionals. Phil O'Donnell, without question, must have learned more about the game in a dozen matches playing alongside a player such as Davie Cooper than he learned in the previous two years.

The Cup-winning team was a perfect blend of experience and youth, and it worked out a treat at the end of the day. It must have given Tommy McLean and Tam Forsyth tremendous satisfaction to see young players such as Chris McCart, Jim Griffin,

O'Donnell and even Tom Boyd and Alastair Maxwell coming through and winning the trophy. It must be very rewarding for them after coaching the players on a daily basis for years – watching them improve and benefit from all the work that has been put in over a long period of time.

The best feature of all is the fact that there is another batch of tremendous prospects, all eager to be given the nod, and year by year the overall situation has constantly improved.

Clubs such as Motherwell simply can't afford to try to compete with the bigger sides who are prepared to spend millions to obtain the services of star players. Motherwell are obliged to do their best to rear their own players. So far it looks as though they are succeeding in achieving their aim to utilise one of the best youth set-ups in the country.

One thing which will come out of the Motherwell Cup victory of 1991 is the fact that quite a few other clubs will take a long, hard look at the financial position they are in and some of them could opt to use Motherwell as their role model. This would entail making a serious commitment to a youth policy because the days are long gone when clubs can risk their future financial stability in order to attempt to keep up alongside the high-flyers. Motherwell, in turn, would need to become even more deeply committed to an already first-class youth policy. To keep ahead of the game will require even heavier involvement. When you hear stories about 13-year-old boys being paid hefty retainers of well over £100 per week to make certain they they will sign on when they become old enough, then you must wonder just exactly where we are heading.

It is a fact that for every boy who makes the grade in professional soccer there are at least another 50 who fail to make the grade and fall by the wayside. It can be a cruel game.

Chapter Nineteen

GROUNDS FOR CONCERN

The impact of the Taylor Report on many football clubs will be catastrophic. It has been decided that every senior football ground must be all-seated by season 1994/95. If the letter of the law is adhered to then this would mean that any area of the ground which is not seated will stand empty during games played at soccer grounds all over the country.

Traditionally, the popular terracing areas of football grounds are where the fans enjoy their matches. The Taylor Report came as a direct result of the Hillsborough disaster and little consideration was taken with regard to the opinions of the fans.

At Fir Park, the enclosure opposite the main stand will be all seated by the end of this summer in readiness for season 1991/92. This area will be known as the East stand.

During the summer break next year the plan will be to build a new grandstand at the south, or visitors', end of the ground. The cost of this stand will be over £1.5 million.

The final phase of the plan to make Fir Park an all-seated stadium will be implemented in the following year. Obviously the costs will be very high and this is at a time when clubs are struggling to meet the financial demands placed upon them in the modern game. Police charges, rates, VAT, etc are among the hidden costs of running a football team and this is before wages, bonus payments, signing-on fees and transfer fees are taken into consideration.

With the overwhelming pressure already upon most clubs there must be a solid case to have VAT taken out of the equation at least during the time when the Taylor Report is being implemented. This 17½ per cent tax on everyone entering the ground should be abolished to allow clubs to use the money which they bring in through their own turnstiles for their own ground improvements.

The possibility also exists that the Scottish Cup final may have to be played at some other venue in the future due to the lack of support by the government for the refurbishment of Hampden. As a traditionalist I deplore the thought of cup finals and inter-national games being played at any ground other than Hampden.

One school of thought is in favour of building a new national stadium in the Strathclyde Park. Those who adhere to this opinion must be easily deluded. If the government fail to support a £40 million project to modernise Hampden how on earth can anyone hold out hope that they will support the building of a brand new stadium which would cost in excess of £80 million?

As for the other alternative, which is to play Cup finals and internationals at Ibrox, well, the paying public let everyone know exactly how they felt about that in the recent friendly international match against Russia which was played at the home of Rangers. A mere 14,000 souls turned up that night to watch Scotland playing. There was absolutely no 'atmosphere' and I for one will restrict my visits to Ibrox to coincide with the occasions when Motherwell are playing there on League or Cup duty in future. I sat shivering with cold at that Ibrox friendly international against Russia and failed to be amused when a thin chant arose from the Copeland Road Stand. A wee knot of Rangers fans were attempt-ing to create some atmosphere as they tried to sing *Flower of Scotland*. The first verse came out something like this:

> Oh flower of Scotland
> When will we see your like again
> Who fought and died for
> The sash my father wore.

No, Ibrox is without doubt a magnificent stadium but along with many others I will give it a body swerve if there is any attempt to utilise it as a replacement for Hampden Park.

What is the answer to this vexed question? Quite simply,

Chris McCart shows his winners medal to a life-long fan

Scottish football will have to get up off its knees, stop begging and whingeing and go out and do it on its own without outside help.

A Hampden lottery should be started right away. Every fan would be able to contribute each week and the proceeds would go into a re-building fund.

A series of international matches could be played with all the proceeds going into the re-building fund. Market the television rights of these games and it is amazing just how much money would accrue. At least that would be a start.

Hampden Park is steeped in tradition and if we allow it to fall into disuse then we will be the ones who have failed Scottish football. It would be dreadful to think that Motherwell's epic Cup final game was one of the last to be played there.

Chapter Twenty

'WELL'S POST-WAR FINALS

Motherwell's games in Cup finals since the war have been strictly limited. On only six occasions have they reached the final stage of Cup tournaments. That, of course, includes the 1991 final. Their record is:

SCOTTISH CUP: PLAYED 3 – WON 2, LOST 1
LEAGUE CUP: PLAYED 2 – WON 1 LOST 1
SUMMER CUP: PLAYED 1 – WON 1

They also won the 1944 Summer Cup but that was DURING the war.

It was back in 1950 that the Motherwell team of that era set about building an enviable Cup reputation. In the early qualifying section the 'Well came out on top against Partick Thistle, Hearts and Airdrie whom they played both home and away. This qualified them for the quarter-finals against Celtic which were again staged at home and away. In the first leg at Parkhead the 'Well scored their biggest Cup victory over Celtic when they destroyed them by four goals to one. The scorers that day were Jim Forrest, Jimmy Watson and Jackie Hunter. The unfortunate Mike Haughney scored an own goal to complete the rout. In the second match at Fir Park big John McPhail hit the 'Well goal-keeper, Dick Hamilton, with an old-fashioned shoulder charge and left him concussed with a badly bruised face (it was a man's game in those days). Celtic won by a single goal but Motherwell went on to the semi-finals by 4–2 aggregate.

Ayr United were the opponents in the semi and a flying right winger called Japp gave the Steelmen a real roasting at Ibrox. With eight minutes left for play 'Well were trailing by 3–1. Wee Johnny Aitkenhead took a hand in affairs at this stage and three late goals saw Motherwell through to face the great Hibernian team in the final. The line up on 28 October 1950 was:

MOTHERWELL	HIBERNIAN
1 JOHNSTONE	1 YOUNGER
2 KILMARNOCK	2 GOVAN
3 SHAW	3 OGILVIE
4 McLEOD	4 BUCHANAN
5 PATON	5 PATERSON (Big Craig's dad)
6 REDPATH	6 COMBE
7 WATTERS	7 SMITH
8 FORREST	8 JOHNSTONE
9 KELLY	9 REILLY
10 WATSON	10 ORMOND
11 AITKENHEAD	11 BRADLEY

Motherwell defended dourly for most of the first half, with the confrontation of Andy Paton and Laurie Reilly being the highlight of the game. Bobby Johnstone, a superb player, created chance after chance for Hibs, but the 'Well defence coped admirably with everything that came their way.

There was no scoring by half time and it stayed that way until the 74th minute when Archie Kelly broke the deadlock. His shot from the edge of the box was partially saved by Younger, who knocked the ball into the air. Archie swiftly followed up and headed the ball over the helpless Tommy Younger into the net.

Two minutes later Willie Watters crossed and Jim Forrest headed home number two.

Tommy Younger fluffed a clearance and it landed at the feet of Willie Watters who was fully 40 yards from goal. Without hesitation he chipped the ball right into the empty Hibs net. The scoreline stood at 3–0 in favour of Motherwell and Andy Paton lifted the Cup to the joy of the 'Well fans in the 64,189 crowd. The odds-on favourites (5–2) had been beaten by the outsiders.

Later on that same season Motherwell knocked Hibs out of the Scottish Cup at the semi-final stage at Tynecastle when they won by 3–2. Archie Kelly had set them on their winning way when he

Andy Paton holds the League Cup aloft. They had just beaten the mighty Hibs team 3–0 in the 1950 League Cup final

scored in 18 seconds. This took Motherwell into their second post-war Cup final.

In that final Motherwell went down to Celtic when they failed to reply to big John McPhail's 13th-minute goal. For the rest of the game, Motherwell pounded the Celtic defence but all their attacks failed to bring any goals due to the finest display of goalkeeping that I have ever seen. John Hunter put up a perfect performance to send the League Cup winners home with the bitter taste of defeat in their mouths.

A year later, Motherwell were back again at Hampden in a Cup final. This was their famous 1952 victory and many, many words have been written and spoken about that epoch-making event. Suffice to say that goals by Watson, Redpath, Kelly and Humphries brought the Scottish Cup to Fir Park for the first time ever.

Two years later, in 1954, in the final of the League Cup

Motherwell players and officials enjoy the champagne after the 1952 final.

John Swinburne with seven of the 1952 Scottish Cup winning team. Left to right: Jimmy Watson, Andy Paton, Tommy Sloan, Charlie Fox, Willie Kilmarock, Archie Kelly and Wilson Humphries

Motherwell met a Hearts team which was to turn out to be one of the finest ever to grace Tynecastle Park. The 'Well defence was at the veteran stage and they failed to match the artistry of the Edinburgh side on that day. The Maroons ran out comfortable winners by 4–2.

Another 11 years were to pass before 'Well graced another final. Bobby Ancell had just left at the end of the 1965 season and Bobby Howitt had taken over as manager. The Summer Cup tournament saw Motherwell against Dundee United in the final. A 3–1 lead was built up at Fir Park before the Steelmen went on to Tannadice to hold out despite a 1–0 defeat and win on aggregate by 3–2.

Chapter Twenty-One

IT WAS A PRIVILEGE TO BE THERE!

After completing the *History of the Steelmen, 1886 to 1986*, I swore that I would never again get involved in a similar project. It had taken five years to write and research that book and while it had proved to be a very successful venture with many pleasant spin-offs, it also had its traumatic moments.

I will never forget, for example, the feeling of panic and self-doubt which assailed me at three in the morning of 10 December 1985 on the day the book was due to be launched. I sat up in bed in a cold sweat. It had cost Motherwell Football Club £11,000 to have the book published and this was at a time when every penny was a prisoner!

'What if nobody buys the book?' I thought. By that time it was far too late to do anything about that and eventually I managed to settle down into a fitful sleep.

As it turned out, the book was very well received and a huge crowd attended the launch in the Motherwell library, including dozens of former players. It was at this launch that the seeds of our Former Players Club were initially sown.

After the Cup final I was approached by Mainstream Publishing and asked if I would undertake to write a book about Motherwell's great victory. The call was well timed because I was still on a 'high' after that great 4–3 result.

'How many words would you require and what's the deadline?' I enquired.

The reply was a bit shattering: '45,000 words and the end of July.'

'Right. That will be no problem,' was my immediate answer and the deal was struck.

It was my intention to write around 1,000 words per night and this would allow me to complete the first draft with about two weeks to spare. At the time of writing – 22 June – I have only about 7,000 words to complete the whole book and I am well ahead of schedule.

I have attempted to link up the start of this book with the end of my last offering and in this way there will be a recorded club history which covers 1886 to 1991.

Basically, this book is a very personal view of a tremendous football match and I have attempted to cover every conceivable aspect of the occasion. There will obviously be the usual errors of omission, for which I freely apologise in advance, but I only hope that, like its predecessor, it becomes 'required reading' for Motherwell supporters and sympathisers.

There is no doubt in my mind that the match itself will go down in the annals of Scottish Football as one of the all-time classics. It had everything from great goals to great goalkeeping, great midfield play and great defending, plus the fact that it was a match which was played in the true spirit of football. Every player on both sides played his part in laying on an exciting, pulsating encounter of the very highest calibre.

The referee may have had his critics in the past but I honestly felt that it was David Syme's very even-handed approach to the game which allowed the play to flow and at the same time kept all the fans in a welter of excitement.

The unfortunate incidents in the tunnel after the final whistle were out of the sight of the viewing fans and therefore did nothing to detract from an occasion which was uniquely satisfying to the supporters of the victors and, to be fair, even the fans of the vanquished team could go home with their heads held high. They had lost yet again but nobody could question their team's determination to go out and have a real go.

Seven goals have been scored in a Scottish Cup final on only four occasions, but the Dundee United v Motherwell epic struggle will live forever in the memories of football fans who were fortunate enough to have been either at Hampden or at least in front of a TV screen. What a tremendous advertisement for the way in which we play football in Scotland. Compare this with the

1991 European Cup final between Red Star Belgrade and Marseilles which was probably THE WORST match seen for many a long year.

Alan Davidson of the Glasgow *Evening Times* eloquently put across the same point in his lead article on the Monday after the Scottish Cup final. He must have the gift of second sight because he forecast that the technical standards of Europe's leading clubs could put the public to sleep. The formula served up at Hampden on 18 May is unbeatable. It gave the fans exactly what they crave for. This was a game which will go down in the annals of Scottish Football as 'The Perfect Final'!

My genuine thanks to the 26 players, three match officials and both management teams for serving up such an exceptionally exciting football match. I doubt if we will ever see its like again . . .

Colin and Stevie enjoy the post-match applause from the fans

APPENDIX: MOTHERWELL STATISTICS 1984–1991

This section lists all the results since Tommy McLean took over as manager in 1984. While this statistics section is not my own idea of good reading, I did find after writing the club's official history that a fair number of fans said that they would have liked to have seen a section devoted to every result in the club's history. As far as I am aware I think that Mr Alex Smith from Bellshill, who did a great deal of early research for me for the centenary book, is intent upon bringing out a statistical reference book which will cover every game ever played by Motherwell FC.

1984/85

First Division

	H	H	A	A
Kilmarnock	W 2–0	D 2–2	D 0–0	
Hamilton Academicals	W 3–0		L 0–2	D 1–1
Partick Thistle	W 2–1		L 1–2	W 1–0
Forfar Athletic	W 2–0		W 2–1	D 0–0
Ayr United	D 1–1		W 3–1	W 2–1
Falkirk	L 2–3		W 3–0	W 2–0
Clydebank	L 0–1	W 1–0	L 1–2	
Meadowbank Thistle	W 3–1	L 0–1	L 2–4	
Airdrie	D 1–1	W 2–0	L 0–2	
Brechin City	W 2–0	W 2–1	W 2–0	
Clyde	D 0–0		D 3–3	L 0–1
East Fife	W 5–0		W 2–1	W 2–1
St Johnstone	L 0–2	W 4–0	W 1–0	

Scottish Cup

Third Round	Dumbarton (H)	W 4–0
Fourth Round	Meadowbank (A)	W 2–0
Quarter-final	Forfar Athletic (H)	W 4–1
Semi-final	Celtic (N)	D 1–1
Replay	Celtic (N)	L 0–3

Skol Cup

Second Round	Ayr United (A)	L 0–1

Top League Scorers: Andy Harrow and Rab Stewart, nine goals each

1985/86

Premier League

	H	H	A	A
Aberdeen	D 1–1	L 0–1	D 1–1	L 2–3
Celtic	L 1–2	L 0–2	L 1–2	L 2–3
Clydebank	D 0–0	W 3–0	D 1–1	D 1–1
Dundee	L 1–3	D 2–2	L 1–3	L 0–4
Dundee United	L 0–1	W 2–0	L 0–3	L 0–4
Hearts	W 2–1	L 1–3	L 0–3	L 0–2
Hibernian	W 2–0	W 3–1	L 0–1	L 0–4
Rangers	L 0–3	W 1–0	L 0–1	L 0–2
St Mirren	W 3–1	L 1–2	L 1–4	L 0–1

Scottish Cup

Third Round	Brechin City (H)	W 2–0
Fourth Round	Alloa (A)	W 2–1
Quarter-final	Dundee United (H)	L 0–1

Skol Cup

Second Round	Partick Thistle (H)	W 1–0
Third Round	Hibernian (A)	L 1–6

Top League Scorer: John Reilly, nine goals

1986/87

Premier League

	H	H	A	A
Aberdeen	L 0–1	L 0–2	D 2–2	L 0–1
Celtic	L 0–4	D 1–1	L 1–3	L 1–3
Clydebank	L 0–1	W 3–2	W 3–2	D 0–0
Dundee	D 0–0	W 2–0	D 1–1	L 1–4
Dundee United	L 0–2	W 1–0	L 0–4	L 0–2
Falkirk	D 2–2	W 1–0	D 1–1	L 0–1
Hamilton	D 1–1	W 3–0	W 3–0	L 2–4
Hearts	L 2–3	L 0–1	L 0–4	D 1–1
Hibernian	W 4–1	W 2–1	D 0–0	W 1–0
Rangers	L 0–2	L 0–1	W 1–0	L 0–1
St Mirren	D 1–1	L 1–2	L 0–1	D 1–1

Scottish Cup

Third Round	Partick Thistle (H)	W 3–1
Fourth Round	Hamilton Academicals (A)	W 2–1
Quarter-final	Hearts (A)	D 1–1
Replay	Hearts (H)	L 0–1

Skol Cup

Second Round	Arbroath (H)	W 4–0
Third Round	Clydebank (H)	W 2-0
Quarter-final	Forfar Athletic (H)	W 2-1 AET
Semi-final	Celtic (N)	D 2-2 Lost 4-5 on penalties.

Top League Scorer: Steve Kirk and Paul Smith, ten goals each

1987/88

Premier League

	H	H	A	A
Aberdeen	L 0–1	W 2–1	L 0–1	D 0–0
Celtic	L 0–2	L 0–1	L 1–4	L 0–1
Dundee	L 0–2	D 3–3	L 0–2	W 2–1
Dundee United	W 2–1	W 4–2	D 1–1	L 1–3
Dunfermline	W 3–2	W 3–2	W 1–0	D 1–1
Falkirk	L 1–2	D 0–0	L 0–3	D 0–0
Hearts	L 0–3	L 0–2	L 0–1	D 1–1
Hibernian	W 1–0	L 0–2	L 0–1	D 1–1
Morton	W 1–0	W 1–0	D 1–1	W 2–0
Rangers	L 0–1	L 0–2	L 0–1	L 0–1
St Mirren	W 2–1	W 2–1	L 0–1	D 0–0

Scottish Cup

Third Round	Kilmarnock (H)	D 0–0
Replay	Kilmarnock (A)	W 3–1
Fourth Round	Dundee (A)	L 0–2

Skol Cup

Second Round	Airdrie (H)	W 3–1
Third Round	Albion Rovers (H)	W 4–0
Quarter-final	Hibernian (H)	W 1–0
Semi-final	Rangers (N)	L 1–3

Top League Scorer: Steve Cowan, nine goals

1988/89

Premier League

	H	H	A	A
Aberdeen	D 1–1	L 0–2	L 1–2	D 0–0
Celtic	L 1–3	D 2–2	L 1–3	W 2–1
Dundee	D 1–1	W 1–0	D 1–1	L 1–2
Dundee United	L 1–2	L 1–2	D 1–1	D 1–1
Hamilton Academicals	D 1–1	W 1–0	L 0–1	W 2–0
Hearts	W 2–0	D 1–1	D 2–2	D 0–0
Hibernian	D 1–1	D 0–0	L 0–1	L 0–2
Rangers	L 0–2	W 2–1	L 1–2	L 0–1
St Mirren	L 1–2	W 4–0	L 0–1	L 1–2

Scottish Cup

Third Round	Falkirk (A)	D 1–1
Replay	Falkirk (H)	W 2–1
Fourth Round	Hibs (A)	L 1–2

Skol Cup

Second Round	Airdrie (A)	W 1–0 AET
Third Round	Dunfermline (A)	L 1–2

Top League Scorer: Steve Kirk, 14 goals

1989/90

Premier League

	H	H	A	A
Aberdeen	D 0–0	D 2–2	L 0–1	L 0–2
Celtic	D 0–0	D 1–1	D 1–1	W 1–0
Dundee	W 3–0	W 3–1	L 1–2	W 2–1
Dundee United	W 3–2	L 0–1	D 1–1	D 1–1
Dunfermline	D 1–1	L 1–3	D 1–1	W 5–0
Hearts	L 1–3	L 0–3	L 0–3	L 0–2
Hibernian	L 0–2	W 1–0	L 2–3	W 2–1
Rangers	W 1–0	D 1–1	L 0–3	L 1–2
St Mirren	W 3–1	W 2–0	D 2–2	D 0–0

Scottish Cup

Third Round	Clyde (H)	W 7–0
Fourth Round	Hearts (A)	L 0–4

Skol Cup

Second Round	Kilmarnock (A)	W 4–1
Third Round	St Mirren (A)	L 0–1

Top League Scorer: Nick Cusack, 11 goals

1990/91

Premier League

	H	H	A	A
Aberdeen	D 0–0	L 0–2	D 1–1	L 0–3
Celtic	W 2–0	D 1–1	D 1–1	W 2–1
Dundee United	L 0–2	W 1–0	L 0–2	L 0–3
Dunfermline	W 2–0	W 1–0	D 3–3	W 5–2
Hearts	D 1–1	L 1–3	L 2–3	L 1–2
Hibernian	W 4–1	W 1–0	L 0–1	D 1–1
Rangers	L 2–4	W 3–0	L 0–1	L 0–2
St Johnstone	W 3–0	D 2–2	L 1–2	W 4–1
St Mirren	D 1–1	W 3–1	L 0–1	D 2–2

Scottish Cup

Third Round	Aberdeen (A)	W 1–0
Fourth Round	Falkirk (H)	W 4–2
Fifth Round	Morton (H)	D 0–0
Replay	Morton (A)	D 1–1 Won 5–4 on penalties
Semi-final	Celtic (Hampden)	D 0–0
Replay	Celtic (Hampden)	W 4–2
Final	Dundee United (Hampden)	W 4–3

Skol Cup

Second Round	Morton (H)	W 4–3
Third Round	Clyde (H)	W 2–0
Fourth Round	Dundee United (A)	L 0–2

Top League Scorer: Dougie Arnott, 14 goals

Motherwell Appearances and Goals

FIRST DIVISION – 1984/85

Player	Apps	Sub	Goals
Ally Maxwell	15	–	–
Andy Dornan	18	(3)	1
Derek Murray	34	–	5
Graeme Forbes	34	(2)	4
Gregor Stevens	8	–	–
Ian MacLeod	38	–	–
Ian MacDonald	10	(3)	4
Gary McAllister	34	(1)	6
Rab Stewart	22	(4)	9
Andy Harrow	36	(1)	9
Kenny Lyall	2	–	–
Paul McFadden	2	(6)	2
Ian Alexander	5	(3)	1
Tom Boyd	35	(1)	–
John Gahagan	17	(14)	5
Ally Mauchlen	29	(1)	1
Michael Cormack	1	(2)	1
Ray Blair	21	(10)	6
Robert Clark	8	(2)	1
Alex Kennedy	14	(2)	2
John Gardiner	24	–	–
Jamie Doyle	15	–	–
Andy Walker	4	(7)	3
John McStay	4	(2)	1

Motherwell Appearances and Goals

PREMIER LEAGUE – 1985/86

Player	Apps	Sub	Goals
John Gardiner	32	–	–
Ian MacLeod	28	(1)	1
Derek Murray	24	(1)	–
John Clark	5	–	–

Alex Kennedy	18	(2)	1
Tom Boyd	31	–	–
Andy Walker	19	(3)	4
Gary McAllister	1	–	–
Andy Harrow	15	(5)	2
Ally Mauchlen	1	–	–
Ray Blair	17	(4)	2
Rab Stewart	3	(4)	1
Jamie Doyle	16	–	–
Andy Dornan	25	(1)	–
John McStay	5	(5)	–
Chris McCart	11	(1)	–
Graeme Forbes	28	–	–
Jim Weir	2	(1)	–
John Reilly	24	(6)	9
Brian Wright	28	(0)	6
John Gahagan	13	(9)	3
Fraser Wishart	26	–	–
Robert Clark	1	(1)	–
Francis Mulvaney	4	(1)	–
Crawford Baptie	14	(2)	3
Jim Griffin	1	–	–
Paul McFadden	–	(1)	–
Ally Maxwell	4	–	–
Martin McBride	–	(1)	–

Motherwell Appearances and Goals

PREMIER LEAGUE – 1986/87

Player	Apps	Sub	Goals
John Gardiner	22	–	–
Fraser Wishart	44	–	3
Derek Murray	13	(7)	–
Alex Kennedy	26	–	1
Graeme Forbes	5	–	–
Tom Boyd	31	–	–
Andy Walker	42	(1)	10
Paul Smith	42	(2)	9
John Reilly	18	(8)	3
Brian Wright	39	(2)	–
Gordon Mair	18	(11)	1
John McStay	2	(2)	–
Gary Fraser	2	(6)	–
Andy Dornan	–	(1)	–
Jamie Doyle	4	(2)	–

John Gahagan	5	(14)	–
Steve Kirk	33	(2)	10
John Philliben	35	(2)	–
Ray Farningham	27	(2)	3
Ally Maxwell	21	–	–
Crawford Baptie	6	(11)	–
Tom MacAdam	31	–	1
Neil Candlish	1	(1)	–
Martin McBride	–	(2)	–
Craig Paterson	16	–	1
Dougie Arnott	–	(1)	–
Kevin McKeown	1	–	–

Motherwell Appearances and Goals

PREMIER LEAGUE – 1987/88

Player	Apps	Sub	Goals
Cammy Duncan	43	–	–
Ally Maxwell	1	–	–
Fraser Wishart	43	–	1
Derek Murray	22	–	–
Craig Paterson	44	–	2
Tom MacAdam	33	(1)	1
Tom Boyd	42	–	2
Jamie Fairlie	8	(4)	1
Steve Kirk	29	(9)	4
Paul Smith	25	(5)	4
Bobby Russell	28	(4)	3
Gordon Mair	16	(5)	1
Ray Farningham	25	(4)	6
John Gahagan	11	(12)	–
Brian Wright	–	(5)	–
Alex Kennedy	–	(1)	–
John Philliben	33	(2)	2
Neil Candlish	7	(2)	1
Gary Fraser	8	(7)	–
Steve Cowan	32	–	9
Martin McBride	4	(6)	–
Mike Caughey	9	(6)	–
Dougie Arnott	–	(2)	–
Jim Griffin	4	(2)	–
Dave Shanks	6	(1)	–
Paul Kinnaird	10	–	–
Chris McCart	–	(1)	–

Motherwell Appearances and Goals

PREMIER LEAGUE – 1988/89

Player	Apps	Sub	Goals
Ally Maxwell	17	–	–
Kevin McKeown	2	–	–
Cammy Duncan	17	–	–
Fraser Wishart	35	–	1
John Philliben	17	(2)	–
Tom Boyd	31	(5)	1
Craig Paterson	33	–	1
Chris McCart	25	(1)	–
Ray Farningham	17	(1)	3
Bobby Russell	28	(3)	5
Paul Smith	3	(1)	–
Steve Kirk	32	(1)	14
Paul Kinnaird	24	–	–
Steve Cowan	12	(7)	2
Martin McBride	10	(6)	1
Tom McAdam	28	–	1
Dougie Arnott	8	(6)	1
Dave Shanks	2	(2)	–
Jim Griffin	1	–	–
Dave MacCabe	12	(1)	–
John Gahagan	10	(4)	2
Gordon Mair	6	(6)	–
Steve Bryce	3	(6)	–
Alex Kennedy	1	–	–
Colin O'Neill	19	–	2
Jamie Dolan	3	(2)	–

Motherwell Appearances and Goals

PREMIER LEAGUE – 1989/90

Player	Apps	Sub	Goals
Ally Maxwell	36	–	–
George Burley	34	–	–
Tom Boyd	33	–	1
Jamie Dolan	5	(7)	–
John Philliben	19	(5)	–
Chris McCart	33	(1)	1
Bobby Russell	32	(1)	3
Colin O'Neill	24	–	1
Nick Cusack	29	(2)	11

Steve Kirk	32	(2)	8
Gordon Mair	7	(2)	–
Dougie Arnott	–	(7)	4
Paul McLean	0	(2)	–
Craig Paterson	33	–	2
Martin McBride	1	–	–
Davie Cooper	31	–	6
John Gahagan	7	(19)	3
Tom McAdam	6	–	–
Mark Reilly	3	(1)	–
Jim Griffen	7	(5)	–
Steve Bryce	–	(3)	–
Dave MacCabe	–	(1)	–
Colin McNair	1	(1)	–

Motherwell Appearances and Goals

PREMIER LEAGUE – 1990/91

Player	Apps	Sub	Goals
Ally Maxwell	36	–	–
George Burley	20	–	–
Tom Boyd	30	–	2
Craig Paterson	28	(5)	2
Luc Nijholt	21	(3)	–
Chris McCart	36	–	–
Bobby Russell	15	(7)	2
Colin O'Neill	21	–	–
Dougie Arnott	26	(3)	14
Steve Kirk	18	(11)	2
John Gahagan	1	–	–
Nick Cusack	22	(7)	4
Jim Griffin	22	(2)	5
John Philliben	11	–	1
Ian Angus	14	(7)	2
Phil O'Donnell	11	(1)	–
Jamie Dolan	4	(5)	1
Joe MacLeod	10	(12)	1
Stevie Bryce	1	(4)	1
Iain Ferguson	13	(2)	7
Gordon Mair	2	–	–
Davie Cooper	34	–	6
Paul McLean	–	(1)	–
Paul McGrillen	–	(2)	–

Motherwell League Appearances under Tommy McLean

Player	Apps	Sub	Goals
Ally Maxwell	130	–	–
George Burley	54	–	–
Tom Boyd	233	(6)	6
Craig Paterson	154	(5)	8
Luc Nijholt	21	(3)	–
Chris McCart	105	(4)	1
Bobby Russell	103	(15)	13
Colin O'Neill	64	–	3
Dougie Arnott	57	(19)	19
Steve Kirk	144	(25)	38
John Gahagan	64	(72)	13
Nick Cusack	51	(9)	15
Jim Griffin	35	(9)	5
John Philliben	115	(11)	3
Ian Angus	14	(7)	2
Phil O'Donnell	11	(1)	–
Jamie Dolan	12	(14)	1
Joe MacLeod	10	(12)	1
Stevie Bryce	4	(13)	1
Iain Ferguson	13	(2)	7
Gordon Mair	49	(22)	2
Davie Cooper	65	–	12
Paul McLean	–	(3)	–
Paul McGrillen	–	(2)	–
Martin McKeown	3	–	–
Cammy Duncan	60	–	–
Fraser Wishart	148	–	5
Kenny Lyall	2	–	–
Gregor Stevens	8	–	–
Ian MacDonald	10	(3)	4
Paul McFadden	3	(7)	2
John Gardiner	56	–	–
Ray Farningham	69	(7)	12
Paul Smith	70	(8)	13
Paul Kinnaird	34	–	–
Steve Cowan	44	(7)	11
Martin McBride	15	(15)	1
Tom McAdam	98	(1)	3
Dave Shanks	8	(3)	–
Dave MacCabe	12	(2)	–
Alex Kennedy	59	(5)	4
John Reilly	45	(15)	12
Colin McNair	1	(1)	–
Jamie Fairlie	8	(4)	1

Derek Murray	93	(8)	5
Neil Candlish	8	(3)	1
Gary Fraser	10	(13)	–
Mark Caughey	9	(6)	–
Graeme Forbes	67	(2)	4
Andy Walker	65	(11)	17
Brian Wright	67	(7)	6
John McStay	11	(9)	1
Jamie Doyle	35	(2)	1
Crawford Baptie	20	(13)	3
Ian MacLeod	66	(1)	1
Robert Clark	9	(3)	1
John Clark	5	–	–
Gary McAllister	35	(1)	6
Andy Harrow	51	(6)	11
Ally Mauchlen	30	(1)	1
Jim Weir	2	–	–
Ray Blair	38	(15)	8
Paul Mulvaney	4	(1)	–
Rab Stewart	25	(8)	10
Andy Dornan	43	(4)	1
Ian Alexander	5	(3)	1
Michael Cormack	1	(2)	1

SCOTTISH FIRST DIVISION: 1984/85

	P	W	D	L	F	A	Pts
1 Motherwell	39	21	8	10	62	36	50
2 Clydebank	39	17	14	8	57	37	48
3 Falkirk	39	19	7	13	65	54	45
4 Hamilton	39	16	11	12	48	49	43
5 Airdrie	39	17	8	14	70	59	42
6 Forfar	39	14	13	12	54	49	41
7 Ayr	39	15	9	15	57	52	39
8 Clyde	39	14	11	14	47	48	39
9 Brechin	39	14	9	16	49	57	37
10 East Fife	39	12	12	15	55	56	36
11 Partick	39	13	9	17	50	55	35
12 Kilmarnock	39	12	10	17	42	61	34
13 Meadowbank	39	11	10	18	50	66	32
14 St Johnstone	39	10	5	24	51	78	25

SCOTTISH PREMIER DIVISION: 1985/86

		P	W	D	L	F	A	Pts
1	Celtic	36	20	10	6	67	38	50
2	Hearts	36	20	10	6	59	33	50
3	Dundee United	36	18	11	7	59	31	47
4	Aberdeen	36	16	12	8	62	31	44
5	Rangers	36	13	9	14	53	45	35
6	Dundee	36	14	7	15	45	51	35
7	St Mirren	36	13	5	18	42	63	31
8	Hibernian	36	11	6	19	49	63	28
9	Motherwell	36	7	6	23	33	66	20
10	Clydebank	36	6	8	22	29	77	20

SCOTTISH PREMIER DIVISION: 1986/87

		P	W	D	L	F	A	Pts
1	Rangers	44	31	7	6	85	23	69
2	Celtic	44	27	9	8	90	41	63
3	Dundee United	44	24	12	8	66	37	60
4	Aberdeen	44	21	16	7	63	29	58
5	Hearts	44	21	14	9	64	43	56
6	Dundee	44	18	12	14	74	57	48
7	St Mirren	44	12	12	20	36	51	36
8	Motherwell	44	11	12	21	43	64	34
9	Hibernian	44	10	13	21	44	70	33
10	Falkirk	44	8	10	26	31	70	26
11	Clydebank	44	6	12	26	35	93	24
12	Hamilton	44	6	9	29	39	93	21

SCOTTISH PREMIER DIVISION: 1987/88

		P	W	D	L	F	A	Pts
1	Celtic	44	31	10	3	79	23	72
2	Hearts	44	23	16	5	74	32	62
3	Rangers	44	26	8	10	85	34	60
4	Aberdeen	44	21	17	6	56	25	59
5	Dundee United	44	16	15	13	54	47	47
6	Hibernian	44	12	19	13	41	42	43
7	Dundee	44	17	7	20	70	64	41
8	Motherwell	44	13	10	21	37	56	36
9	St Mirren	44	10	15	19	41	64	35
10	Falkirk	44	10	11	23	41	75	31
11	Dunfermline	44	8	10	26	41	84	26
12	Morton	44	3	10	31	27	100	16

SCOTTISH PREMIER DIVISION: 1988/89

		P	W	D	L	F	A	Pts
1	Rangers	36	26	6	4	62	26	56
2	Aberdeen	36	18	4	14	51	25	50
3	Celtic	36	21	11	4	66	44	46
4	Dundee United	36	16	8	12	44	26	44
5	Hibernian	36	13	14	9	37	36	35
6	Hearts	36	9	14	13	35	42	31
7	St Mirren	36	11	18	7	39	55	29
8	Dundee	36	9	17	10	34	48	28
9	Motherwell	36	7	16	13	35	44	27
10	Hamilton Academicals	36	6	28	2	19	76	14

SCOTTISH PREMIER DIVISION: 1990/91

		P	W	D	L	F	A	Pts
1	Rangers	36	24	5	7	62	23	55
2	Aberdeen	36	22	5	9	62	27	53
3	Celtic	36	17	12	7	52	38	41
4	Dundee United	36	17	12	7	41	29	41
5	Hearts	36	14	15	7	48	55	35
6	Motherwell	36	12	15	9	51	50	33
7	St Johnstone	36	11	16	9	41	54	31
8	Dunfermline Athletic	36	8	17	11	38	61	27
9	Hibernian	36	6	17	13	24	51	25
10	St Mirren	36	5	22	9	28	59	19